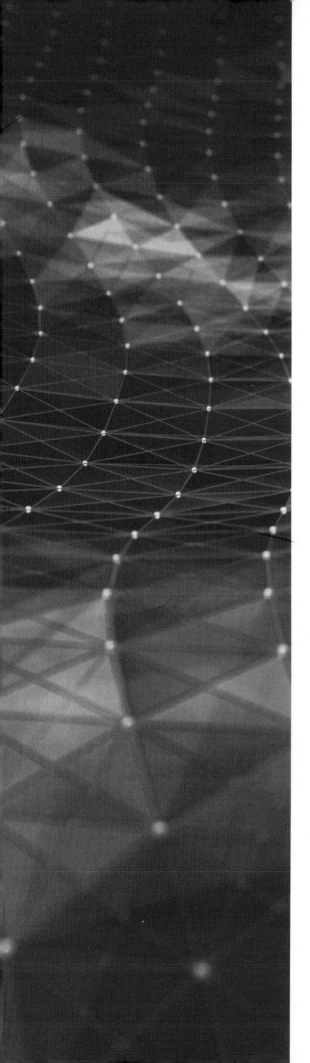

Client Money and Assets

Edition 5, September 2021

This learning manual relates to syllabus
version 5.0 and will cover examinations from
11 December 2021 to 10 December 2023

APPROVED WORKBOOK

Welcome to the Chartered Institute for Securities & Investment's Client Money and Assets study material.

This manual has been written to prepare you for the Chartered Institute for Securities & Investment's Client Money and Assets examination.

Published by:
Chartered Institute for Securities & Investment
© Chartered Institute for Securities & Investment 2021
20 Fenchurch Street
London EC3M 3BY
Tel: +44 20 7645 0600
Fax: +44 20 7645 0601

Email: customersupport@cisi.org
www.cisi.org/qualifications

Author:
Chris Selden BSc(Hons), Chartered MCSI

Reviewers:
Dominic Collinson Hollinghurst, Chartered FCSI
Austin Copp, Chartered MCSI

This is an educational manual only and the Chartered Institute for Securities & Investment accepts no responsibility for persons undertaking trading or investments in whatever form.

While every effort has been made to ensure its accuracy, no responsibility for loss occasioned to any person acting or refraining from action as a result of any material in this publication can be accepted by the publisher or authors.

A learning map, which contains the full syllabus, appears at the end of this manual. The syllabus can also be viewed on cisi.org and is also available by contacting the Customer Support Centre on +44 20 7645 0777. Please note that the examination is based upon the syllabus. Candidates are reminded to check the Candidate Update area details (cisi.org/candidateupdate) on a regular basis for updates as a result of industry change(s) that could affect their examination.

The questions contained in this manual are designed as an aid to revision of different areas of the syllabus and to help you consolidate your learning chapter by chapter.

Please note that, as part of exam security, handheld calculators are not allowed in CISI exam venues. Candidates must use the onscreen calculator for all CISI CBT exams in all languages in the UK and internationally.

Learning manual version: 5.1 (September 2021)

Learning and Professional Development with the CISI

The Chartered Institute for Securities & Investment is the leading professional body for those who work in, or aspire to work in, the investment sector, and we are passionately committed to enhancing knowledge, skills and integrity – the three pillars of professionalism at the heart of our Chartered body.

CISI examinations are used extensively by firms to meet the requirements of government regulators. Besides the regulators in the UK, where the CISI head office is based, CISI examinations are recognised by a wide range of governments and their regulators, from Singapore to Dubai and the US. Around 50,000 examinations are taken each year, and it is compulsory for candidates to use CISI workbooks to prepare for CISI examinations so that they have the best chance of success. Our workbooks are normally revised every year by experts who themselves work in the industry and also by our Accredited Training Partners, who offer training and elearning to help prepare candidates for the examinations. Information for candidates is also posted on a special area of our website: cisi.org/candidateupdate.

This workbook not only provides a thorough preparation for the examination it refers to, it is also a valuable desktop reference for practitioners, and studying from it counts towards your Continuing Professional Development (CPD). Mock examination papers, for most of our titles, will be made available on our website, as an additional revision tool.

CISI examination candidates are automatically registered, without additional charge, as student members for one year (should they not be members of the CISI already), and this enables you to use a vast range of online resources, including CISI TV, free of any additional charge. The CISI has more than 40,000 members, and nearly half of them have already completed relevant qualifications and transferred to a core membership grade. You will find more information about the next steps for this at the end of this workbook.

It is estimated that this manual will require approximately 50 hours of study time.

What next?
See the back of this book for details of CISI membership.

Need more support to pass your exam?
See our section on Accredited Training Providers.

Want to leave feedback?
Please email your comments to learningresources@cisi.org

Before you open Chapter 1

We love a book! ...but don't forget you have been sent a link to an ebook, which gives you a range of tools to help you study for this qualification

Depending on the individual subject being studied and your device, your ebook may include features such as:

Watch video clips related to your syllabus

Read aloud function*

Adjustable text size allows you to read comfortably on any device*

Pop-up definitions

Highlight, bookmark and make annotations digitally*

Images, tables and animated graphs

Links to relevant websites

End of chapter questions and interactive multiple choice questions

* These features are device dependent. Please consult your manufacturers guidelines for compatibility

CHARTERED INSTITUTE FOR SECURITIES & INVESTMENT

The use of online videos and voice functions allowed me to study at home and on the go, which helped me make more use of my time. I would recommend this as a study aid as it accommodates a variety of learning styles.

Billy Snowdon, Team Leader, Brewin Dolphin

Find out more at cisi.org/ebooks

An Introduction to Client Money and Assets

Introduction 3

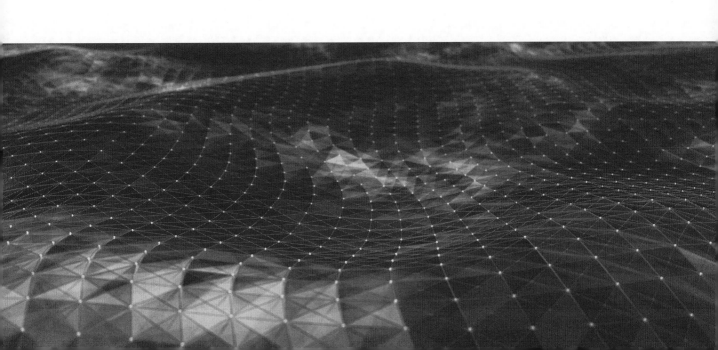

Introduction

The study of Client Money and Assets differs from many of the other aspects of regulation that are explored in the Investment Operations Certificate (IOC) workbook series, and understanding this at the outset will probably be useful to students.

The Client Assets (CASS) Sourcebook (which contains the **Financial Conduct Authority (FCA)** Rules) is applicable to many different types of **firm**, and so must cover many different business processes and types of service. The CASS Sourcebook also contains a wide range of types of rule – some requiring very precise and specific treatments and controls, others set out the 'big picture' requirements while leaving firms with flexibility to design and implement their own approaches relative to the type of financial services and products they offer and the types of clients they support.

This gives firms great freedom – but the specific rules cover such a range of potential services that the rules can at times lose clarity. Each firm should, therefore, ensure that it has understood the CASS rules at a holistic level, understanding which of the various elements are relevant and which are not, and how the firm's selected approach provides compliance with the rules that are relevant to it.

However, as we will see, this flexibility has made the drafting of individual rules more difficult (in contrast to the FCA prescribing by rule a single operational approach that all firms would be obliged to follow). Many rules become harder to interpret as a result, and some can appear to be contradictory. Therefore, each firm will at times need to make and document its own decision as to how a given rule should be interpreted to suit its context – in light of its own control environment and the services it provides.

Each firm should be able to clearly and confidently explain its position to its regulator or **auditor** (who we will see plays a very important role in ensuring that firms are acting within the CASS rules). However, the auditor must in turn recognise that there is no single 'solution' to client money and asset controls. The auditor should be able to test the way in which each firm has established its control framework according to its own interpretations of what CASS requires of it. Indeed, practitioners will be aware that different audit firms may hold differing views on a number of topics. What matters is that firms are not expected to fit into a single mould – an outcome that would reject the flexibility the FCA has rightly written into the rules. Rather, CASS compliance requires an active engagement by all participants to ensure that a logical model reflecting the rules has indeed been implemented by each firm, and is operating as designed.

The auditor should be able to determine whether the overall controls implemented by a given firm successfully combine to satisfy the specific requirements of the CASS rules, ie, to assess whether a firm is compliant in its approach, rather than inadvertently imposing a common approach on all firms they review. It is vital that the firm is able to clearly and consistently communicate how the decisions regarding its CASS controls relate to the actual business being undertaken, and that the auditor approaches its review of each firm based on the actual business model being serviced.

The dynamic that this situation creates has a significant impact upon the writing of a workbook on CASS. For example, it is not appropriate or helpful to provide fully detailed examples of how a reconciliation should be completed, because the rules support multiple approaches and different administration systems will create different reporting extracts. As such, this workbook will primarily focus upon the rules and guidance. Guided by the syllabus it will unpack the background behind why certain controls are required, and highlight some reasons why different types of firm might approach a given control in different ways. In this way we should be able to understand both the specific requirements of the individual rules while also understanding the broad purpose for which those rules were created – to protect **client assets** (usually described as 'the spirit of the rules'). However, if a firm's view of 'the spirit of the rules' would conflict with multiple actual rules, it would seem difficult to justify that perspective.

What remains is for you, as a CASS practitioner in whatever role and type of company you serve, to:

- remain alert to the balance between prescription and flexibility within the CASS rules
- understand the way in which your organisation has interpreted the client money and asset rules, and
- be able to confidently demonstrate (both to internal and external audiences) the holistic rationale by which the CASS controls established in your organisation satisfy the specific requirements of the CASS rules.

Our hope is that this workbook will help prepare you for that challenge.

Chapter One
Fundamentals of Client Money and Assets

This syllabus area will provide approximately 4 of the 50 examination questions

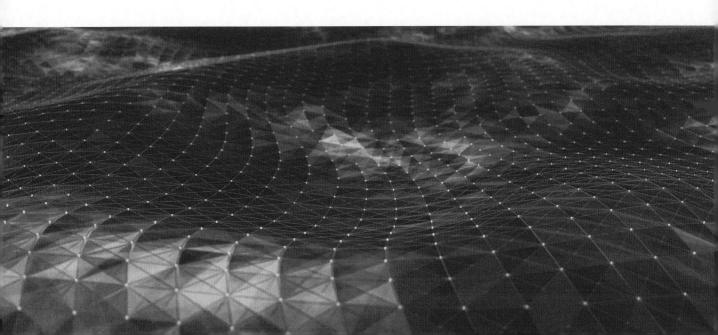

1. Fundamentals of Client Money and Assets

Learning Objective

1.1.1 Understand the objectives of the UK CASS regime and the interaction with the FCA's statutory objectives

1.1 Giving Confidence to Clients

To be successful, the financial services sector needs a number of strong foundations to be in place. At an overall industry level, these foundations are secured through the work of the Financial Conduct Authority (FCA) – in its role as one of the national regulators.

The FCA has a strategic objective to ensure that the relevant markets are functioning well. This is supported by three operational objectives:

- **protect consumers** – secure an appropriate degree of protection for consumers
- **protect financial markets** – protect and enhance the integrity of the UK financial system
- **promote competition** – promote effective competition in the interests of consumers.

These together should produce an environment in which consumers can have confidence that financial firms will perform in the expected ways, and that firms both understand and manage the structural risks associated with achieving those client outcomes.

It is, therefore, particularly important that consumers can be confident that a regulated firm will take good care of any money or assets held on behalf of the consumer, and the Client Assets Sourcebook (CASS) sets out the FCA's requirements on regulated firms in this regard.

While CASS is important in how a relevant firm runs its business at all times, the potential risks for a consumer are perhaps best illustrated by considering the potential consequences if a firm was to become insolvent while holding assets of its clients.

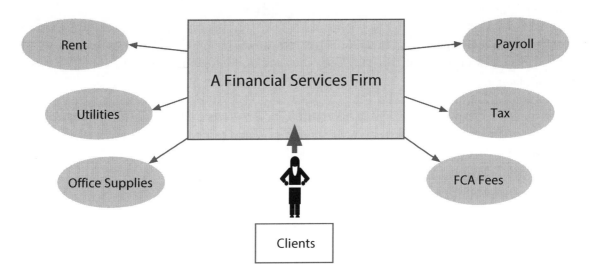

A financial services firm is a business like any other, incurring a range of expenses as illustrated in the above diagram. Its income comes from the fees and charges or dealing profit it collects from its clients in return for the services provided.

However, if the client's money was simply received by the firm into its own corporate accounts, then that money would be mixed within all other assets of the firm. In the event of insolvency, the creditors of the firm would be able to claim against all these as assets of the firm. In this way, the firm's insolvency would put the clients at risk.

For this reason, each regulated firm must segregate the money and assets of its clients from its own corporate money, and the CASS rules set out in detail exactly how such **segregation** is achieved. The principle is that the firm creates a distinct set of records specifically recording client positions (separate from any corporate assets held), and establishes separate bank accounts. Similar arrangements apply to clients' assets covered in custody arrangements under which assets of its clients will be held. In this way, the firm creates a segregated environment in which assets of its clients are secure.

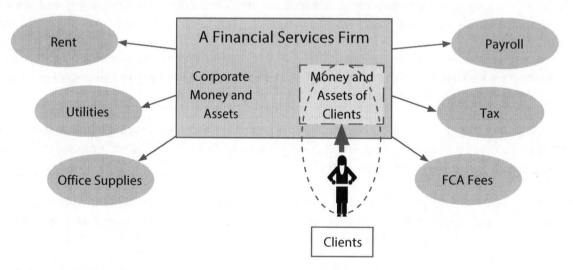

In the event that the firm goes out of business, this segregation protects the clients' assets from the firm's creditors. If a company can no longer pay debts as they fall due, the legal process of insolvency begins. Insolvency sees a specialist party (known as an insolvency practitioner) take effective control of the failing company to either:

a. solve any underlying problems and rescue the company to continue as a going concern; or
b. wind up what remains of the company's activities and distribute the realised assets between its creditors.

In the event that a regulated firm was to enter insolvency, the segregated assets are protected for the benefit of the firm's clients. The insolvency practitioner would respect that client assets could not be sold in order to pay the corporation's general creditors. In this way, the clients are protected against the risks of the firm's insolvency.

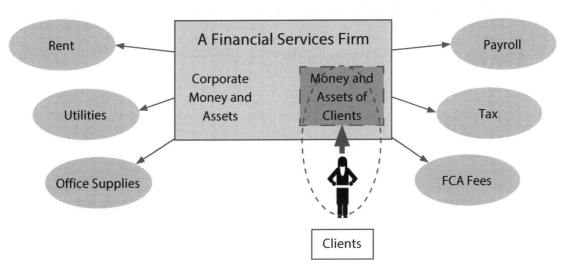

There are some important points to note about this premise. Firstly, it is important that each separate regulated firm (ie, each legal entity) establishes its own segregation arrangements. Secondly, the segregation process must be robust enough to withstand any legal challenge. This requires the segregation to be achieved both practically (through the use of specific client accounts) and legally (by evidencing that the party holding the assets on behalf of the firm recognised that the assets held in those accounts were not corporate assets).

1.2   Giving Confidence to Clients

Learning Objective

1.1.2   Know the importance of legal entity separation

The controls and processes required by the CASS rules must be established by each regulated firm. In some cases this is simple to achieve, where the firm's investment offering is limited, and the firm is independent of other financial services firms and is maintained in isolation. However, there are many large financial services organisations which comprise multiple separate regulated firms. In such cases, the management of each regulated firm in the organisation must ensure that the CASS rules are followed for their firm on a standalone basis.

It is not acceptable for a larger organisation to blur the boundaries between multiple legal entities within its broader group structure (indeed, such blurred responsibilities have at times been cited by the FCA when penalising firms for inadequate CASS controls). Clients enter into legal agreements with a specific firm, and that firm has a corresponding duty to protect its clients' assets. In the event of insolvency affecting all or part of a larger financial services organisation, there must be no ambiguity over who are the clients of the affected legal entities and which clients are not affected because they have no relationship with the specific legal entity becoming insolvent.

2. Legal Contracts and Relationships

2.1 Components of a Contract

Learning Objective

1.2.1 Understand the importance of client agreements

Everything that a regulated firm does for its client is a matter of legal contract – and so it is useful to have an understanding of how contracts are formed.

Four things are required to form a legal contract:

1. Offer (ie, an offer by one party to provide goods or services to another party, based on certain specified terms and conditions).
2. Acceptance (ie, confirmation by the second party that it agrees with the offer made).
3. 'Valuable consideration' (a contract needs some form of payment, as otherwise it is simply one party helping another. This 'payment' might not be in money, but it must be something that is agreed as valuable).
4. An intention by both parties to enter into a legally binding agreement (normally evidenced by a written contract being negotiated and signed by both parties).

2.2 Formation of Client Contracts

If we consider a simple example: suppose you offer to look after my garden while I am on holiday, and I say 'yes, thank you'. If we do not agree any form of payment then no legal contract would be created – it is simply you doing me a favour. If you, however, had expected me to pay you and you then tried to sue me for non-payment, the courts would not support your claim. There is also no evidence that we both intended to form a legally binding contract.

If we extend the example, suppose you run a window-cleaning business and have put an advert in the local paper, to which I reply. In law, your advertisement is not an 'offer' but is instead called an 'invitation to treat'. If I reply to your advertisement asking you to work for me, I am making the offer. At some point you would tell me what you would charge, and the terms of that 'valuable consideration' are wrapped up in the offer I make (ie, I want you to clean my windows once a month in return for a specified payment). You would check whether you are able to take my job (you might already be fully booked, or my house may be too far away for you to want to take on my business) and you would then agree to my offer. Being a professional, you would probably want us to have some documentation confirming the agreement – because you would want to be protected against me later trying to avoid payment, or claiming that you had not done the agreed work.

We can apply this model to a financial services relationship. Let us imagine a firm called 'Dependable Investments ltd'. It publishes marketing material to advertise its services and a potential client finds those services appealing.

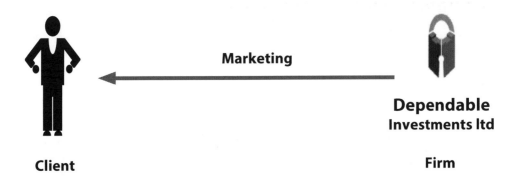

The client reads the terms and conditions defining the service, and completes the application form (making an offer to the firm to enter into a legal contract defined by those terms and conditions).

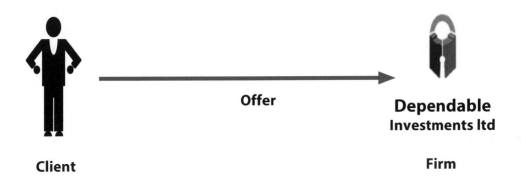

The firm will check that the application has been correctly completed, that the person appears to satisfy any eligibility requirements for the service (such as a minimum age, or minimum investment value, or satisfactory completion of anti-money laundering checks) and, if satisfied, will agree to provide the service and so the legal relationship begins.

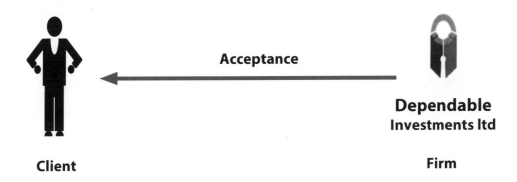

The CASS rules that we will explore in this workbook are applicable to a wide range of firms and servicing relationships, and firms must ensure that their actions and records are aligned with the services they are providing. The fundamental aspects of legal contracts discussed above provide an important foundation for the treatment of client assets.

2.3   A Financial Services Transaction

You will have noted from the window-cleaning example that goods or services are passed from one party to the other, while 'valuable consideration' flows in the opposite direction. While a legal contract is formed each time a client takes up a service from a regulated firm, each separate **transaction** performed within that service is also a legal 'contract'.

It is important to recognise that CASS is focused upon the books and records of the assets and money that a firm holds on behalf of its clients, and the firm's controls over those assets and records. CASS rules do not consider the quality and speed with which a firm executes the client's instructions (other parts of the FCA rules address such points), and do not need the firm to specifically calculate future balances based on pending transactions. CASS rules must be approached from the perspective of what assets and money *are* held, and what assets and money the firm's records indicate *should* be held for each client. An understanding of the transaction life cycle is therefore important to each firm building a cohesive approach to complying with the CASS rules.

Consider a simple example: a client purchasing units in a collective investment scheme (CIS) via an investment platform.

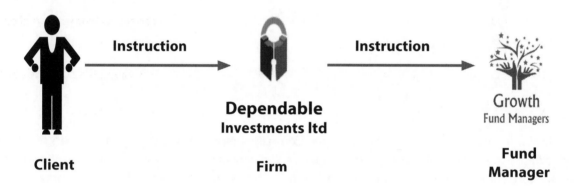

The client has a relationship with Dependable Investments ltd ('Dependable') (the investment platform firm), and instructs it to buy units in a fund operated by Growth Fund Managers ltd ('Growth'). Dependable will usually combine that order with any other orders it receives for that same fund, and will instruct an aggregated deal for the Growth fund. The terms of the deal are agreed, and this date is known as the 'trade date'.

'**Settlement**' of the deal follows a number of days later. For many funds, settlement occurs three days after trade date (known as 'T+3'). 'Settlement date' is the date on which the valuable consideration on the contract becomes due, and legal ownership of the asset will be expected to transfer in full to the new owner (subject to any relevant terms and conditions). Up until settlement date, the transaction contract could therefore still fail, as either party might fail to deliver the money or assets required by the contract. On settlement date, the transfers and exchanges should be completed.

However, even the simple example above demonstrates that there is more than one contract at work. The client only has a contract with 'Dependable', and has no direct relationship with 'Growth'. 'Dependable' has entered into two different contracts.

1. a client contract to allocate the asset to the client's account (providing the client pays the necessary valuable consideration to 'Dependable'), and
2. a fund manager contract to purchase the actual units from 'Growth' (which bears a settlement obligation for 'Dependable' to pay on settlement date).

Trading in equities or corporate bonds and other securities would follow a similar journey, though the period between 'trade date' and 'settlement date' may be different, so firms supporting a range of products must ensure they understand the applicable settlement obligations.

Note that the two transactions are related to the extent that 'Dependable' is only trading with 'Growth' fund managers because its client placed an order. However, they each form separate contracts and so 'Dependable' is obliged to settle its transaction with 'Growth' fund managers even if some problem prevents the client's money from being received.

All types of business models need to recognise these aspects, and the potential misalignment of settlement is a key factor behind the complexity of the CASS rules. The CASS rules do not tell firms how to resolve the practical difficulties, but they do ensure that the consequences of such problems are addressed in order to minimise the overall risks that clients experience loss as a result.

The multiple transactions taking place also illustrate two other important aspects of controlling client money and assets:

*   the importance of maintaining detailed books and records, so that the firm knows the status of each transaction it has undertaken, and
*   the importance of being clear which legal entity is concerned in any given transaction.

2.4   Two Approaches to Settlement

Learning Objective

1.2.2   Understand the difference between contractual and actual settlement and the key implications for client assets segregation: transfer and other settlement systems

As noted above, each transaction has a contractual settlement date (ie, the agreed date on which the cash and securities executed by the trade are exchanged to reach settlement), but problems can prevent actual settlement from being completed on that date. For example:

*   if the valuable consideration is not transferred to the seller, or
*   if a physical asset is not delivered to the buyer.

Such situations expose the parties to legal claims because the terms of the contract have not been satisfied. While the specific management and resolution of such legal claims fall outside the scope of this workbook, it is important to note one way in which the industry seeks to manage the potential consequences of a failed settlement. Remember that the market at its heart operates by moving the same assets between different owners at agreed contractual prices. The same asset might be scheduled to settle between multiple parties on the same date. Therefore, a failure by one party to complete any transaction on any day could produce a wave of failures for other firms (for example, Firm A cannot deliver the asset to Firm B because it did not receive it from Firm C.)

While 'actual settlement' reflects the position summarised above (by which settlement occurs at the point when parts of the transaction are actually completed), many firms adopt an approach known as 'contractual settlement' to support their services.

'Contractual settlement' simply means that the firm honours the terms of the original contract. If a firm offers contractual settlement to its client, it will record the asset bought as being available for the client's use with effect from the contractual settlement date of the purchase transaction – irrespective of any upstream failed settlement, ie, the firm reflects to its client that the settlement was completed as intended. A firm that offers contractual settlement of trades therefore takes on a financial risk; by telling its client that an asset purchase has been successfully completed, the client might instruct the sale of that asset. If the firm did not actually receive the asset now being sold, it will not only need to resolve that problem, but must also now deliver the relevant sale proceeds to its client. (Offering contractual settlement also has implications for the firm's CASS reconciliations, which we will consider in chapter 5.)

Contractual settlement, therefore, creates financial exposures for the firm, but does simplify aspects of its market and customer interactions. Each firm will make its own decision as to whether to provide contractual settlement, and will need to write the necessary information into its operational processes and the terms and conditions which govern its services. It should be noted that, in some cases, a firm might provide contractual settlement for only a small number of days (intended to provide the typical additional time necessary to resolve any problem in effecting trade settlement).

3. Looking after Assets for Clients

Learning Objective

1.3.1 Know that the UK operates a trust regime and other types of regime (agency and custodial regimes)

1.3.2 Understand the fundamental concepts of trust law, including the concept of fiduciary duty, statutory trust, and pollution of the trust

1.3.3 Know how legal title is registered and recorded

3.1 The Custodian Regime

We have already mentioned a couple of different types of financial services firm (investment platform providers and fund managers). However, when considering market settlement and the security of client assets, a key type of firm is the **custodian**.

This is a specific type of regulated firm which exists in order to hold assets on behalf of its clients – and will settle market trades on their behalf.

Generally, a custodian will operate a large market position, ie, an aggregated holding representing all of its various clients. Historically, these records became known as 'nostro' and 'vostro' accounts.

In the same way that 'nous' in French means 'us', the custodian's 'nostro' account represents its own overall position. It is the internal record that the custodian maintains of what has actually happened.

'Vostro' means 'yours' (as in 'vous' in French), and the custodian's 'vostro' account is the position that it tells each client is held for their account.

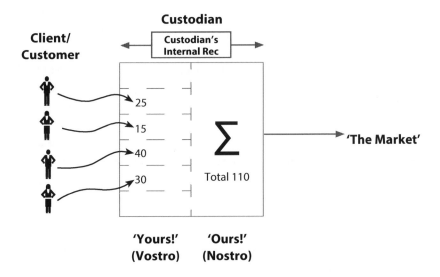

(The Greek letter 'sigma' (Σ) is mathematical shorthand for 'the sum of', as used in spreadsheet software.)

Importantly, it is the custodian's responsibility to ensure that any difference between its nostro and vostro positions is identified and resolved. The custodian's client is able to simply rely upon the vostro position that the custodian reports (as the custodian is telling the client that the associated money and assets are available for their use).

It should be noted that a platform provider (such as 'Dependable' in the example above) will also have a nostro and vostro position. On the one hand, 'Dependable' is ensuring that its market activity is correctly recorded; on the other hand, it is providing each customer with a record of the assets that 'Dependable' considers are available to trade.

Alignment of these two internal views (nostro and vostro) is therefore an important control, as we will see later in the workbook.

3.2   Registration of Assets

We began by emphasising the need for a client's assets to be segregated from any assets of the firm. We, therefore, need to understand how ownership of transferable securities (such as shares, bonds, and units in collective investment schemes (CISs) is demonstrated. Historically, companies issued physical share certificates to investors who bought shares in the company. However, in order to enable computerised trading of securities, share certificates were largely replaced by electronic registers (a process known as 'dematerialisation'). Ownership of most types of financial instrument is now evidenced in the electronic 'register' of that asset.

The register is a record maintained by the company (or some other party that has issued the asset to the market) in which the number of shares/units owned by each person is recorded.

The person or institution named in the register is called the registered owner, and is said to own 'legal title' to the asset (assuming that any obligations under the contract to buy the asset have been satisfied).

If each client bought the asset directly from the issuer, then each person would be directly recorded on the register of that asset and the client would directly hold 'legal title' to that asset. However, the financial services sector provides products and services to clients in ways intended to simplify the process for clients or to reduce the risks associated with direct investment. As such, transactions will often include additional parties, and various firms retain the services of other specialist companies in order to support their business models.

The inclusion of additional firms within the chain of ownership of an asset often means that the assets are not registered in the name of the individual client. As most financial assets are registered, it is important that the way any firm holds assets demonstrates that client assets are separate from any corporate assets it also holds.

While assets could be registered in the name of the individual underlying client, this would not be effective for some business models and product requirements. Therefore, it is common for a financial services firm to use a **nominee** company to hold client positions.

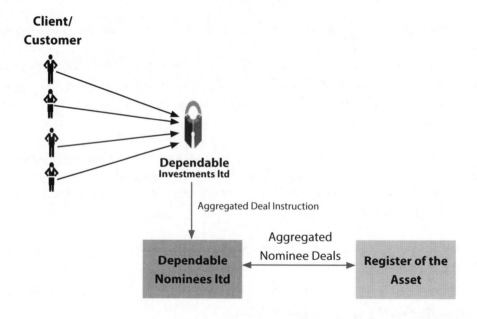

A nominee company is a distinct legal entity used to hold assets that must not perform any other business activity or trading. As a result, in the event that Dependable Investments ltd was to become insolvent, the separate nominee company 'Dependable Nominees ltd' would not be drawn into that insolvency (as the nominee company simply exists to hold the segregated positions on behalf of the operating company). A nominee company has no FCA authorisation as it performs no regulated services. It simply exists to provide a different legal entity to act as registered owner for assets that need to be segregated. The regulated firm will maintain internal records for the assets.

In respect of most assets, the CASS rules expect assets to be held in either the client's name or the nominee company of either the firm or an authorised third party custodian. We will consider in chapter 5 the additional options that CASS allows for assets traded in certain non-UK markets.

3.3 The Statutory Trust Regime

English law recognises another legal structure that can support segregation, which is used in particular to ensure the legal segregation of **client money**. This structure is the statutory trust regime. We will see that CASS rules themselves create a legal 'trust', enabling a legal entity (eg, 'Dependable Investments ltd') to open a bank account that is legally separate from any other bank account opened in its own corporate name, ie, rather than using a nominee or other company to act in a custodian capacity, the trust regime provides a legal segregation that is reflected within the records of the legal entity.

A key foundation of English trust law is the role of the trustee – the person who holds an asset on behalf of another. We see this trustee role in various contexts: unit trusts, pension trusts, and bespoke trusts that people may create for their own affairs and inheritance management. Regardless of the context, the trustee of a trust must always act solely in the interests of the beneficiaries (the people for whose benefit the trust is established). The important consideration for CASS is that client money is held under statutory trust (rather than the firm simply acting in its clients' interests to protect their assets).

For a firm to successfully maintain the statutory trust to provide the necessary segregation of client money, it is necessary to ensure that the trust arrangement has legal standing, to provide a sufficiently robust legal protection of client money against claims from other creditors of the firm in the event of the firm's insolvency. It is, therefore, vital that the bank (or other third party) holding the money in the client bank account acknowledges that the trust exists. We will consider the 'trust acknowledgement letters' used to recognise this legal segregation in more detail in chapter 3 of this workbook. Note that to be effective, both legal and physical segregation are required.

Any failure to maintain the correct physical segregation can undermine the validity of the trust. Therefore, if a bank account covered by the client money statutory trust was found to contain corporate money of the firm, the trust might fail and all the money held within that account could be claimed for general creditors by an insolvency practitioner. Such a blurring of segregation is sometimes referred to as 'pollution of trust'.

In respect of client money, it is therefore important that a firm only puts corporate money into a client money bank account in the specific circumstances when CASS permits or requires it to do so. Putting corporate money into a client money bank account under any circumstance not set out in the CASS rules could pollute the trust and so undermine the protection of client money.

End of Chapter Questions

Think of an answer for each question and refer to the appropriate section for confirmation.

1. What are the Financial Conduct Authority's (FCA's) operational objectives?
   Answer reference: Section 1.1

2. What is the overarching aim of the Client Assets Sourcebook (CASS) rules?
   Answer reference: Section 1.1

3. Why is it important for a large services organisation to ensure that CASS rules are satisfied for each separate legal entity within the group?
   Answer reference: Section 1.2

4. Each legal entity must ensure segregation of client assets from the firm's own assets. What two aspects of this segregation must both be in place to ensure it is effective?
   Answer reference: Section 1.1

5. What are the four legal stages in forming a contract?
   Answer reference: Section 2.1

6. What is meant by 'contractual settlement' and what is the implication for the client where a firm provides 'contractual settlement'?
   Answer reference: Section 2.4

7. In general, where is ownership of a transferable security recorded, and what is the impact where an investment business holds those assets for their clients?
   Answer reference: Section 3.2

8. What is a nominee company?
   Answer reference: Section 3.2

9. What effect does trust law have on the holding of client money?
   Answer reference: Section 3.3

10. What could be the consequence if the firm failed to maintain correct segregation?
    Answer reference: Section 3.3

Chapter Two
Regulatory Structures

This syllabus area will provide approximately 6 of the 50 examination questions

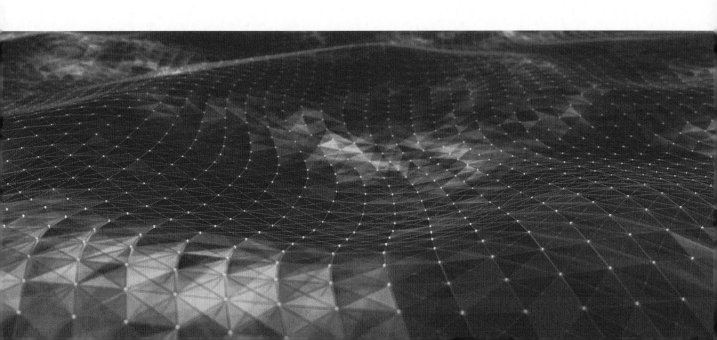

1. The Financial Conduct Authority (FCA) and its Rules

Learning Objective

2.1.1 Understand the meaning and purpose of the elements of the FCA Handbook that are relevant to client assets protection, including: the FCA Principles for Business (PRIN); Senior Management Arrangements, Systems and Controls (organisational arrangements) (SYSC); CASS Sourcebook; Conduct of Business Sourcebook (COBS); Supervision (SUP); Compensation (COMP)

1.1 The FCA Handbook and its Sourcebooks

The FCA regulates financial services firms in the UK. Each firm wanting to perform certain types of activity (such as giving investment advice, dealing in investments, or acting as a custodian) must apply to the FCA for permission to perform those services, as it is illegal to perform regulated business in the UK without first being authorised by the FCA. Each legal entity that is authorised receives a set of permissions (which are publicly visible via the FCA's website: https://register.fca.org.uk).

Once authorised, the firm must operate in line with the requirements of the FCA Handbook, which is also available via the FCA's website (https://www.handbook.fca.org.uk/). The Handbook is very large and covers a wide range of areas. To help firms navigate the rules, and to help each firm identify the parts of the Handbook that are relevant to its own blend of regulatory permissions, the Handbook is split up into a set of Sourcebooks (each of which is known by an abbreviation).

Each Sourcebook provides the FCA's rules for a given subject area – whether these rules are decided specifically by the FCA, or are rules which are applicable in the UK because of our national participation in various international conventions (or which remain aligned with rules made by the European Union (EU)).

The following table summarises a number of Sourcebooks and the role they fulfil:

Sourcebook	Full Name	Role
PRIN	Principles for Businesses	Sets out 11 overarching principles that govern the way in which a firm should operate. For example, Principle 10 requires that 'A firm must arrange adequate protection for clients' assets when it is responsible for them.'
SYSC	Senior Management Arrangements, Systems, and Controls	This mainly focuses on the actions of a firm's senior management while running the regulated firm. SYSC contains requirements for governance arrangements, and the ways a firm should oversee 'outsourcing' (the situation where a regulated firm retains regulatory responsibility for its work, but delegates to a third party the performance of underlying administrative tasks).
COBS	Conduct of Business Sourcebook	Contains detailed requirements regarding the way that various tasks should be completed – particularly the firm's interactions with its clients. COBS includes rules for categorising clients as retail, professional, or counterparties; it prescribes various communications that the firm should provide at various stages during a business relationship (such as providing trade confirmation information having agreed the terms of a contract on trade date and providing statements). COBS also includes obligations on the firm to act honestly, fairly and professionally in accordance with the best interests of its client. This overarching requirement covers a range of activities, for example, not making improper profits out of the client's investment activity.
CASS	Client Assets	Detailed rules regarding identification, segregation, and controls to protect client money and custody assets.
SUP	Supervision	Sets out how the FCA will achieve active supervision of regulated firms. SUP sets out various reports that a firm must submit to its regulator (including the '**Client Money and Assets Return**', known as 'CMAR'), as well as confirming how a firm can change the set of permissions it holds (for instance, if the firm wants to open up a new business activity). SUP Chapter 3 sets out important requirements in relation to the firm's auditors.
COMP	Compensation	While 'compensation' is often associated with rectification after a complaint or an error by the firm, the COMP sourcebook outlines the workings of the **Financial Services Compensation Scheme (FSCS)**. Regulated Firms have obligations in respect of FSCS activity (including confirming the qualifying conditions for an claim, recognising eligible claimants, and time limits on payments). The role of FSCS will be discussed in chapter 8 of this workbook.

Other Sourcebooks set out the requirements for firms to hold a sum of capital in reserve to reduce the risk of the firm becoming insolvent without notice, and specific rules for firms that operate regulated collective investment schemes (CISs) or act as a credit union. However, the Sourcebooks listed in the table are the most relevant to defining how the firm must ensure the protection of client money and custody assets.

1.2   FCA Principles for Business

It is useful to be familiar with the 11 FCA Principles for Businesses, as they provide a high-level basis for the underlying specific rules contained in the other Sourcebooks. While Principle 10 is specifically addressed at clients' assets, a number of other Principles are relevant to the way in which a firm ensures that the risks associated with its client responsibilities are appropriately managed.

	Principle	'A firm must...'
1	Integrity	...conduct its business with integrity
2	Skill, care and diligence	...conduct its business with due skill, care and diligence
3	Management and control	...take reasonable care to organise and control its affairs responsibly and effectively, with adequate risk management systems
4	Financial prudence	...maintain adequate financial resources
5	Market conduct	...observe proper standards of market conduct
6	Customers' interests	...pay due regard to the interests of its customers and treat them fairly
7	Communication with clients	...pay due regard to the information needs of its clients and communicate information to them in a way which is clear, fair and not misleading
8	Conflicts of interest	...manage conflicts of interest fairly, both between itself and its customers, and between customers and other clients
9	Customers: relationships of trust	...take reasonable care to ensure the suitability of its advice and discretionary decisions for any customer who is entitled to rely upon its judgement
10	Clients' assets	...arrange adequate protection for clients' assets when it is responsible for them
11	Relations with regulators	...deal with its regulators in an open and cooperative way and must disclose to the FCA appropriately anything relating to the firm of which the FCA would reasonably expect notice

1.3   Individual Sourcebook Rules

Each Sourcebook contains many rules – the COBS Sourcebook is over 500 pages long if printed in full – so each Sourcebook is split into chapters containing numbered sections. Any individual rule can be identified by using the Sourcebook, chapter number, section number, and paragraph number. For example, below is an extract from the CASS Sourcebook (correct as of August 2021) introducing the external client money reconciliation.

		External client money reconciliations
7.15.20	R	A *firm* must conduct, on a regular basis, reconciliations between its internal records and accounts and those of any third parties which hold *client money*. [**Note**: article 2(1)(c) of the *MiFID Delegated Directive*]
7.15.21	G	The purpose of an *external client money reconciliation* is to ensure the accuracy of a *firm's* internal records and accounts against those of any third parties by whom *client money* is held.

We will discuss reconciliations in detail later in this workbook. At this point, let's focus upon the way the Handbook works.

The rule references are shown on the left-hand side. 7.15.20 identifies the 20th paragraph of the 15th section of the 7th chapter of the Sourcebook (which in this case is CASS).

The 'R' denotes a 'Rule'. This is a requirement, something that the firm must do (if the context of that rule is applicable to the business undertaken by the firm). In the case above, any firm that uses a third party to hold client money would be required to perform this reconciliation. Note however that a rule will often be written in a way that sets a principle or an objective, rather than prescribing the individual steps that the firm must take. This is deliberate, in order to provide the maximum possible flexibility to firms to make their own business decisions rather than being squeezed into a single mould.

This is where other types of paragraph become relevant. In the above extract, CASS 7.15.21 has a letter 'G' rather than a letter 'R'. The 'G' stands for 'Guidance': additional comments to help the firm understand and apply a specific rule. In this case, the guidance focuses on the practical purpose of the reconciliation rule. A firm can devise an external client money reconciliation in line with its own business structures – but if that reconciliation process fails to achieve the purpose stated in the guidance then the firm might later be found to have breached the rule to which that guidance relates. Note that on a technical point a firm cannot breach guidance; it can however breach a rule if it has not sufficiently satisfied any relevant guidance associated with that rule.

Most of the Handbook is made up of rules and guidance, though there are some other types of content, as shown in the following extract from CASS Chapter 10.

10.1.9   [E] (1) For the purpose of ▪ CASS 10.1.7 R, the following documents and records should be retrievable immediately:

    (a) the document identifying the institutions referred to in ▪ CASS 10.2.1R (2);

    (b) the document identifying individuals pursuant to ▪ CASS 10.2.1R (4);

    (c) any written notification or *acknowledgement letters* referred to in ▪ CASS 10.2.1R (5);

    (d) the most recent *internal custody records checks* referred to in ▪ CASS 10.3.1R (3);

    (e) the most recent *external custody reconciliations* referred to in ▪ CASS 10.3.1R (5);

    (f) the most recent *internal client money reconciliations* referred to in ▪ CASS 10.3.1R (7) and ▪ CASS 10.3.1R (7A); and

    (g) the most recent *external client money reconciliations* referred to in ▪ CASS 10.3.1R(7A).

  (2) Where a *firm* is reliant on the continued operation of certain systems for the provision of component documents in its *CASS resolution pack*, it should have arrangements in place to ensure that these systems will remain operational and accessible to it after its insolvency.

  (3) Contravention of (1) or (2) may be relied upon as tending to establish contravention of ▪ CASS 10.1.7 R.

'E' denotes an 'Evidential Provision'. This is a specific form of guidance which produces a regulatory 'safe-zone'. Where a firm can show it has satisfied an evidential provision, that fact is deemed to demonstrate compliance with the associated rule (where normal 'guidance' paragraphs will usually still leave some space for interpretation). Note that the above is not itself a rule, and so the firm would not be obliged to complete the six items listed. However, if the firm can demonstrate that these six points have been met, the firm will be seen as having satisfied CASS 10.1.7R (as noted in the opening sentence).

There are some other types of paragraph in the FCA Handbook, but these are rare and so will not be discussed in this workbook.

You may have noted that some words in the above Handbook extracts are in italic font. This identifies terms that have been specifically defined by the FCA in the Handbook glossary. Some definitions are detailed and complex; others are simply used to establish a term that can be referenced within a number of other Handbook paragraphs.

2. FCA Authorisation and Permitted Business

Learning Objective

2.2.1 Understand the scope of regulated activities which could give rise to client assets

2.2.2 Know the geographical application of CASS rules

2.2.3 Know which permissions could give rise to client money obligations

2.2.4 Know how permission to hold client money is granted

2.2.5 Know the difference between holding client money and deposit taking

2.2.6 Understand the application of the banking exemption

The Financial Services and Markets Act 2000 (FSMA) is the primary legislation that sets out the regulatory structures for UK financial services. It is supported by various other legal materials, including the Regulated Activities Order (RAO), which establishes the specific types of activity that can only be performed by a firm holding the relevant FCA authorisation.

Each firm must therefore consider its intended business model and services against two lists arising from the RAO:

- **regulated activities** – the firm must identify which (if any) of these activities it will be performing, and
- **specified investments** – the firm must determine which of these investment types will be applicable to each of the activities it will undertake.

The firm will then seek FCA authorisation for the resulting scope of its business. Such firms may be domiciled in the UK or in other countries, but in order to perform regulated activities within the UK market, any firm must first gain authorisation from the FCA – even if that firm is already authorised by another regulator in its home country.

2.1 Activities

The FCA is responsible for regulating over 60 different activities, though many of these are slight variations of others. The following table is not therefore exhaustive, but it summarises a number of broad areas covered by these activities, and lists some actual activities as examples. We will discuss many of these permissions in more detail as the workbook continues.

Broad Area	Comment	Example FCA Activity
Dealing in investments	Relevant for a firm which will be party to transactions (as agent or **principal**)	Dealing in investments as agent Dealing in investments as principal

Broad Area	Comment	Example FCA Activity
Arranging investments	Being a key part of a process that results in investments taking place, though without being a 'party' to the investment contracts	Arranging (bringing about) deals in investments Making arrangements with a view to transactions in investments
Investment Management	Directly making investment decisions on behalf of a client, in respect of that client's portfolio	Managing Investments
Responsibility for a Collective Investment Scheme (CIS)	Acting as the operator or trustee of a CIS, with different management activities applying to different types of CIS	Managing an undertakings for collective investment in transferable securities (UCITS) Managing an authorised Aternative Investment Fund (AIF) Acting as trustee or depositary of a UCITS Acting as trustee or depositary of an AIF
Financial Advice	Giving advice to a client about the best financial decisions to take in their circumstances	Advising on Investments Advising on regulated mortgage contracts Providing 'basic advice' on stakeholder products
Custody	Either looking after the assets of a client, or bringing about the context in which a third party will directly look after the assets of your client	Arranging safeguarding and administration of assets Safeguarding and administering of assets (without arranging)
Insurance	Permissions relating to firms writing insurance, but also permissions related to other firms involved in the operation of insurance (such as claims management)	Effecting contracts of insurance Carrying out contracts of insurance Assisting in the administration and performance of a contract of insurance
Permissions relating to debt services	Being professionally or officially engaged in managing or resolving a situation of debt, mainly in respect of consumer credit, either on behalf of the consumer or the creditor	Debt adjusting Debt counselling Debt collecting

As you can see, the regulatory perimeter covers a large number of activities, and so the FCA is responsible for regulating a diverse range of companies.

One practical consequence of this is that some aspects of the Handbook (such as CASS) have become more complex due to the increased diversity that the rules need to govern. Each FCA-regulated firm – whether domiciled in the UK or overseas – must determine which parts of CASS are applicable to its business model and operations.

In respect of each activity, the firm will also state whether the activity will be performed for retail clients, professional clients, or eligible counterparties. This all forms part of the firm's permission statement.

You will also note that performing the types of activity listed above could result in the firm at some point receiving or holding the money of its client, in order to efficiently complete the client's instructions. A financial adviser may instruct and settle transactions; a debt management service may receive its client's money in order to give confidence to the client's creditors; the authorised fund manager (AFM) of a regulated CIS will normally receive money from unitholders and ensure unit redemption proceeds are sent back to unitholders.

2.2   Specified Investments

The full list of specified investments contains over 20 different types of financial asset. However, for the purposes of this workbook the most relevant are listed below:

*   contracts of insurance
*   shares
*   fixed-income securities, gilts or bonds
*   rights to or interests in investments
*   units in a CIS
*   financial futures
*   options
*   contracts for differences.

When requesting authorisation from the FCA, the firm must confirm which specified investments will be applicable to each activity it intends to operate.

2.3   Deposits and Deposit-taking

In addition to the items listed above, there is one additional activity and one further specified investment that we must consider. There is an activity for 'accepting deposits', which is the activity of receiving money from a client in order to hold it as banker. This permission is therefore only applicable to credit institutions, such as licensed banks, and relates to the context where money is held on the bank's own balance sheet to support a loan book or for other purposes.

The activity of accepting deposits is used in respect of the specified investment of 'deposits'. This can be viewed as money that has been consciously deposited with a specific bank in order to bring about the benefits offered by that **deposit** (eg, to earn interest, or gain access to banking services). This is different from client money, which the rules define as being money relating to the investment business being undertaken.

For that reason, the permissions discussed above do not refer to client money, because 'money' is not a specified investment, and each activity must relate to specified investments. It is, however, important to know whether a firm is permitted to hold client money, and so the firm's overall statement of permissions will include a comment from the FCA confirming whether or not the firm is allowed to hold client money. When drawing up its business model in readiness for submitting an authorisation request to the FCA, the firm will determine whether it will need to handle client money in order to provide its services to customers – and the FCA will consider this request as part of the overall authorisation process.

It also follows that where a firm has permission to take deposits, it is able to consider any money received from/for its clients as being a deposit held for those clients as opposed to a sum of uninvested client money held on behalf of those clients. As such, the CASS 7 rules for handling client money need not be applied to a bank in respect of money it is holding as a deposit taker. This is sometimes referred to as 'the banking exemption' (though the CASS Sourcebook itself does not use the term). In such a position, when the firm chooses to use this exemption, it is necessary for the bank to disclose to clients the fact that the money will be held as banker rather than being protected under the client money rules. If the bank decides to protect the money as client money, it must also disclose this to the clients, so that there is clarity over which arrangements apply.

2.4 An Example Permission Statement

All of the points discussed above (activities, specified investments, and ability to hold or control client money) come together in the firm's permission statement. The permissions held by each regulated firm can be seen in the FCA Register (accessed via the FCA website). While outside the scope of this workbook, it should be noted that many permission statements will include a 'Requirement' (agreed between the firm and the FCA as being relevant to the firm's business).

Here is an extract of a firm's permission statement, accessed via the FCA website:

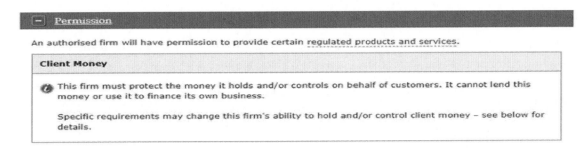

Arranging safeguarding and administration of assets

Customer Type
Retail (Investment)

Investment Type
Certificates representing certain security

Debenture

Government and public security

Rights to or interests in investments (Security)

Share

Unit

Warrant

Limitation
Investment activity in

Arranging (bringing about) deals in investments

Customer Type
Eligible Counterparty

Investment Type
Certificates representing certain security

Contract for Differences (excluding a spread bet and a rolling spot forex contract)

Debenture

Future (excluding a commodity future and a rolling spot forex contract)

Government and public security

Life Policy

Option (excluding a commodity option and an option on a commodity future)

Rights to or interests in investments (Contractually Based Investments)

Rights to or interests in investments (Security)

Share

Unit

Warrant

Note that the above example shows the wording used when a firm is allowed to hold client money. Where a firm is not permitted to hold client money the following text will be used:

Client Money

 This firm cannot hold client money. It may be able to control client money if it has the necessary requirements.

Where a firm is authorised to accept deposits, the permission statement will include an element such as the following:

Accepting Deposits

Customer Type
All

Investment Type
Deposit

It is therefore possible for a credit institution to obtain both the 'accepting deposits' permission and the 'client money' permission. However, these permissions relate to fundamentally different treatments of money:

* Client money is segregated from the firm's money.
* Deposits are received onto the bank's balance sheet.

Therefore, the two approaches would not be used together in respect of the same money.

3. Roles and Responsibilities

Learning Objective

2.3.1 Know the roles and responsibilities of the following in relation to client assets protection: the FCA; authorised firms that hold or control client money or assets; SMF Prescribed Responsibility 'z'; auditors

2.3.2 Know the classifications of authorised firms as per CASS 1A

Successful protection of client assets across the industry requires a number of parties to fulfil specific functions. Each of these responsibilities is complementary to ensure overall protection for clients and confidence in the market.

At this point, we will discuss the roles of these parties at a high level. Later in this workbook we will explore these roles in greater depth and discuss the practical realities.

3.1 The FCA

The FCA's primary responsibilities in respect of client asset protection are to authorise firms and to maintain the Handbook of rules and guidance in a way that enables firms to appropriately minimise risk and to ensure that firms meet the FCA's expectations through supervision and enforcement. In respect of client assets, we will naturally focus on the rules within the Client Assets Sourcebook.

CASS is split into 14 chapters (each covering a different aspect of client assets) supported by additional schedules and a set of transitional provisions (relating to rule changes). These are listed in the following table:

Section	Heading	Section	Heading
CASS 1	Application and general provisions	CASS 12	Commodity futures trading Commission Part 30 exemption order
CASS 1A	CASS firm classification and operational oversight	CASS 13	Claims management: client money
CASS 3	Collateral	CASS 14	Temporary Permissions Regime – client assets rules
CASS 5	Client money: insurance mediation activity	TP	Transitional provisions
CASS 6	Custody	Sch 1	Record-keeping requirements
CASS 7	Client money	Sch 2	Notification requirements
CASS 7A	Client money distribution	Sch 3	Fees and other required payments
CASS 8	Mandates	Sch 4	Power exercised
CASS 9	Information to clients	Sch 5	Rights of action for damages
CASS 10	CASS resolution pack	Sch 6	Rules that can be waived
CASS 11	Debt management: client money		

The chapters relevant to an individual firm will depend upon the types of business undertaken. For example, a firm that has no involvement in insurance services will not be subject to any rules in CASS 5. Similarly, CASS 6 is normally only relevant to a firm that provides services relating to **safe custody assets**. This workbook focusses on firms conducting investment business in the UK, and therefore only the most relevant chapters of CASS are covered.

It is important to note that while the chapters are distinct there are important crossovers between the different chapters, because the rules relate to transactions and record-keeping which by definition will often involve questions of whether a given client is entitled to an asset or the corresponding transaction settlement proceeds. It is therefore important that the CASS rules are approached as a whole, because approaching single rules in isolation (without then surveying the overall position) can lead to misunderstanding or misapplication of controls.

It must also be recognised that the CASS rules are written with a sense of realism. CASS does not expect perfection or the total removal of risk; rather it defines certain controls that a firm must introduce to ensure that any risks will be mitigated and that errors will be identified and rectified. For example, CASS 7 includes requirements for the performance of client money reconciliations – and sets out how the firm should resolve any discrepancies that arise. The fact that a discrepancy arises is not always a breach of CASS, though failure to manage that identified discrepancy within the necessary time period would be a specific CASS breach (we will look at reconciliations in detail later in the workbook).

It must also be recognised that CASS does not specify every individual control that a firm should implement. CASS covers a wide range of financial services, so requires each firm to ensure that it implements organisational arrangements adequate for that firm's activity. While CASS specifies a number of key controls, and in some cases prescribes those controls in great detail, the CASS rules grant firms much flexibility in many areas regarding the way in which the firm chooses to perform its business.

It is the FCA's role to ensure that the right degree of flexibility is available, and that the CASS rules clearly set out the regulator's expectations. If the CASS rules are unclear then there will be inconsistency regarding how different firms approach a given topic.

3.2 Authorised Firms

We have seen that each authorised firm needs to determine what types of permitted business it will undertake, and apply for the relevant authorisation. Once operational, the firm must ensure that its business decisions and operational processes are compliant with CASS.

We have noted that while the CASS rules are very detailed in many areas, the rules also contain much flexibility over the way that a firm decides to structure its business processes. To give a simple illustration (though we will address the full rules in more detail later, as there are some exemptions that need to be considered), the rules require client money to be segregated from corporate money of the firm, with that segregation continuing during any period in which the firm is effecting a payment back to its client (such as where the client has requested the sale of an asset and the withdrawal of the sale proceeds). While the firm might achieve this by effecting the outward payment from a **client bank account (CBA)** (an account to hold money segregated as client money per CASS), CASS also allows the firm to effect the payment from a corporate account – provided an equal amount remains segregated in a CBA until the payment is completed.

This simplified example illustrates that the CASS rules allow firms to arrange their accounting and transactional processes in a number of ways. As such, there is no single means of complying with CASS. It is therefore necessary that each firm understands the consequences of each choice it makes – however trivial an individual choice might initially appear – to ensure that the consequences of those choices do not breach specific obligations under CASS. The firm must also recognise that any resulting CASS tensions may not indicate that the relevant rule is faulty or inadequate, but may instead arise from some decision made earlier in its business design process. If so, the firm should explore how changing that earlier decision would enable compliance with CASS and/or be ready to clearly explain and justify its position.

It is also worth noting that under the CASS rules (specifically CASS 1A) each firm will be categorised according to the highest value of client money and/or safe custody assets held by the firm in the last calendar year. The following table summarises the parameters that determine which category is applicable to a firm:

CASS Firm Type	Client Money: Highest amount held in last calendar year (or projected for current calendar year)	Safe Custody Assets: Highest value held in last calendar year (or projected for current calendar year)
CASS Large Firm	More than £1 billion	More than £100 billion
CASS Medium Firm	Between £1 million and £1 billion	Between £10 million and £100 billion
CASS Small Firm	Less than £1 million	Less than £10 million

Some firms may hold client money; others may hold safe custody assets; some will hold both. If a firm holds both types of asset for its clients, its categorisation will be the higher of the two results. For example, if the firm held no more than £5 million of client money at any time in the last calendar year, but held safe custody assets with a peak value of £120 billion during that period, the firm would be a CASS large firm by virtue of its safe custody asset position, despite its client money balance only categorising the firm as a CASS medium firm.

The categorisation of the firm affects how certain control obligations apply to a firm, and these will be noted as the workbook progresses. It will also impact the level of focus the FCA gives the firm.

3.3   SMF Prescribed Responsibility 'z'

The FCA places specific obligations on the individuals performing the most senior activities within a regulated firm. The Senior Managers & Certification Regime (SM&CR) covers executive directors and other key roles (such as the MLRO), with additional specific responsibilities being recognised as a firm increases in size.

A firm subject to CASS must identify its most senior leader responsible for the performance of CASS activity (usually a board member), and formally allocate to that individual prescribed responsibility 'z' (which relates to compliance with CASS). This person then has direct responsibility to the FCA to the appropriateness of the firm's CASS policies and practices, and can be penalised by the FCA if deficiencies are found.

In many firms there will be a separate person (or team) working for this individual to perform CASS operational oversight and provide findings and information to the person holding prescribed responsibility 'z'. (The topic of CASS operational oversight will be discussed further in chapter 7).

3.4   Auditors

All public companies are required to retain an independent auditor to ensure that their corporate accounts are properly maintained. This is equally true for financial services firms, though certain firms are also subject to a separate obligation to have an annual assurance process carried out by auditors, to check and report on their compliance with the CASS rules.

These CASS audit reports are provided to the FCA and so it is important for the firm to ensure that its CASS assurance process is completed on time. There is of course potential for firms and auditors to have differing views as to whether a certain aspect of the firm's approach is compliant with the requirements of CASS, and such discussions can be highly technical. It is therefore important for the firm to articulate the overall business approach and the implications of the individual matter under discussion to the auditor's satisfaction.

4.   International Considerations

So far we have built up the foundations of client asset obligations from the basis of a UK company operating within the UK market under UK rules. However, the growth of international trading means that the UK model does not sit in isolation. There are three main themes to consider:

- A UK firm that wants to sell its services in other countries.
- A non-UK company that wants to sell its services within the UK.
- The effect of international rules upon the FCA Handbook.

4.1   European Regulations and Directives

Learning Objective

2.4.1   Understand the general requirements of UK MiFID as they relate to client assets protection

2.4.2   Know the general requirements of the Insurance Distribution Directive relating to client money

Most relevant to such discussion is the status of the UK as a former member of the EU. The EU enables the free movement of goods and services between EU member states, which is supported by an agreed set of EU Regulations and EU Directives.

Technically, an EU Regulation is a directly binding law applicable to all EU member States, while an EU Directive is an agreed approach that each member state should separately write into its domestic statutes.

There are a large number of EU Regulations and Directives, and the most important with relevance to client assets are as follows:

- Markets in Financial Instruments Directive (MiFID), and
- the Insurance Distribution Directive (IDD).

The UK's decision to leave the EU means that such rules are no longer imposed on the UK, and over time, we can expect UK and EU rules to diverge to some extent. However, at present, UK statute strongly reflects the EU rules. For example, the obligations on EU firms arising under MiFID are effectively still applicable in the UK under a combination of primary and secondary legislation referred to as 'UK MiFID'.

From a CASS perspective, however, the historic origin of any particular measure is now of less importance, as the FCA will decide upon future changes to CASS without being directly bound by decisions taken in the EU. References to MiFID and other EU rules do however remain within the FCA Handbook.

CASS rules derived from EU Regulations/Directives are often written as high-level expectations, such as the following examples:

7.12.1	R	**Requirement to protect client money** A *firm* must, when holding *client money*, make adequate arrangements to safeguard the *client's* rights and prevent the use of *client money* for its own account. [**Note**: article 16(9) of *MiFID*]
7.12.2	R	**Requirement to have adequate organisational arrangements** A *firm* must introduce adequate organisational arrangements to minimise the risk of the loss or diminution of *client money*, or of rights in connection with *client money*, as a result of misuse of *client money*, fraud, poor administration, inadequate record-keeping or negligence. [**Note**: article 2(1)(f) of the *MiFID Delegated Directive*]

The above rules emphasise that each firm must have adequate arrangements in place to minimise the risk of loss of client money, but they are only expressed at a high level, and the specific controls that a firm must establish as part of these overall adequate arrangements (such as the external client money reconciliation noted above) are set out in other areas of CASS. In the situation where a firm has failed to consider its overall control environment, the firm may be in breach of the above high-level rules.

There can be a situation where a firm has established what it considered to be adequate organisational arrangements and subsequently discovers a flaw in those arrangements. The firm should investigate the issue and take appropriate steps to remediate its arrangements to ensure they are again *'adequate… to minimise the risk of loss…'*. Such a response to the discovery would align with the expectations of this rule (though there may be debate as to whether the existence of the discovered deficiency itself constituted a breach of this particular rule, providing the firm acts promptly to resolve the concern). If however the identified weakness meant that a specific CASS control (such as the external client money reconciliation) had not been correctly completed for a period, the firm would record a breach against such a specific failing.

Another EU Directive that remains relevant to the protection of client assets in the UK is the Insurance Distribution Directive (IDD), which sets out requirements for firms that fulfil supporting functions in respect of insurance business. Note that the IDD does not affect the activities of the insurer itself; it relates to the firms which enable that insurance contract to operate. The IDD sets out requirements relating to how any insurance premiums passing through **agents** or brokers need to be segregated to protect clients against insolvency.

4.2   Passporting

The most significant benefit of harmonised EU rules is the ability for a firm domiciled and regulated in one member state to offer its services in another member state without needing to become authorised in that second member state. This ability to operate across EU borders on the strength of a single authorisation is known as passporting.

Passports are not however applicable where an EEA-regulated firm wants to offer services in a country outside the EEA, or when a non-EEA firm wants to offer services within the EEA. In such cases, full domestic authorisation would be required, and the relevant rules therefore applied.

The UK's decision to leave the EU therefore means that:

- any UK firm wishing to provide financial services in another EU country must obtain any necessary authorisation from the regulator of the country concerned (and FCA permissions can no longer be passported into the EU), and
- any non-UK firm wishing to provide financial services in the UK must be authorised by the FCA, regardless of any similar authorisation that firm has already obtained in another EU Member State.

End of Chapter Questions

Think of an answer for each question and refer to the appropriate section for confirmation.

1. What does the Senior Management Arrangements, Systems, and Controls (SYSC) Sourcebook govern?
   Answer reference: Section 1.1

2. Which sourcebook of the Financial Conduct Authority (FCA) Handbook requires a firm to act in the best interests of its clients?
   Answer reference: Section 1.1

3. What is the most relevant of the Principles for Businesses (PRIN) and how does it apply to client assets?
   Answer reference: Section 1.2

4. What is the Financial Services and Markets Act (FSMA) and what does it mean to client assets?
   Answer reference: Section 2

5. How do firms obtain the authority to hold client money and safe custody assets?
   Answer reference: Section 2

6. What activities related to client assets require firms to be approved and regulated?
   Answer reference: Section 2.1

7. What is the difference between deposit-taking and holding money as 'client money'?
   Answer reference: Section 2.3

8. What is the 'banking exemption' and how does it impact relevant firms?
   Answer reference: Section 2.3

9. Under CASS 1A, what are the criteria for a firm to be classified as a CASS medium firm?
   Answer reference: Section 3.2

10. How does the client assets regime reflect the Markets in Financial Instruments Directive (MiFID)?
    Answer reference: Section 4.1

Chapter Three
Client Money Fundamentals (CASS 7)

This syllabus area will provide approximately 9 of the 50 examination questions

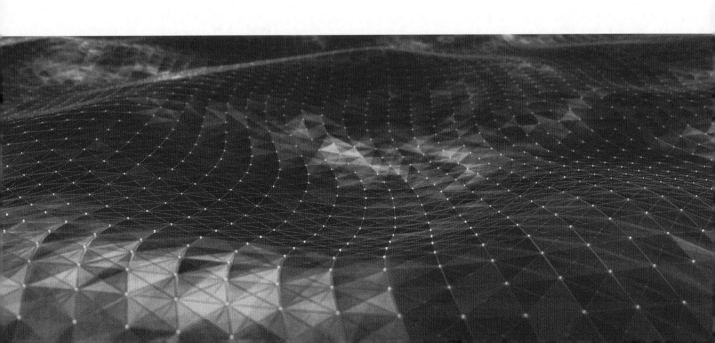

1.   Client Money: What It Is

In this chapter we will build on the foundations discussed in earlier chapters, with a focus on client money. The first step is therefore to establish exactly what constitutes 'client money'.

The Financial Conduct Authority's (FCA's) glossary definition of 'client money' is complicated, largely because the definition is written in terms of the different types of regulated business that a firm might undertake. For the purposes of this workbook, we will adopt a different approach, which aligns with this definition but enables us to more readily see the key stages in determining whether or not a sum of money received by the firm should be considered to be 'client money' or not.

There are two broad categories of money that should be treated as client money under the rules of CASS 7 (Chapter 7 of the CASS Sourcebook). The first broad category relates to money that is moving between legal entities as part of enabling investment activity. The following will serve as our abridged definition to determine amounts as being client money:

- *'Money…*
- *…that a firm receives…*
- *…from its client or for its client…*
- *…in connection with designated investment business (and certain other types of FCA-regulated business)*
- *…unless a CASS 7 exemption is applied.'*

When considering any process flow, the firm should consider whether the above five elements are satisfied. Looking at these elements enables some important observations to emerge:

- Client money rules relate to money. If the firm receives something other than money, CASS 7 is not applicable. (While this might initially seem an obvious point, we will see that there are some circumstances where the firm will need to check whether the thing it has received is 'money' or something else.)
- Money from/for a client is not client money until it is received by the firm. The firm has no CASS 7 responsibility for money it has not yet received.
- Money that is received but which the firm can show does not relate to a client cannot be client money, so should no longer be segregated.
- Money that passes between the firm and its client but is not related to the investment activity being undertaken would fall outside of CASS 7.
- There are a number of exemptions written into CASS 7, which a firm can consider when drawing up its business model. We will return to exemptions later, once the fundamental approach and controls have been discussed.

The second category of money that needs to be understood in respect of CASS 7 is money that the rules specifically instruct (or in some cases permit) the firm to treat as client money, even though it does not satisfy the five points above. Where the above describes the position where money is moving between parties, this second category relates to situations requiring the firm to take some of its corporate money and treat it as client money. Importantly, the firm cannot simply decide to treat money as client money; it can only segregate corporate money as client money in response to a specific CASS 7 rule. Treating corporate money as client money in any other case risks polluting the trust established to protect money.

2. Segregation of Client Money

We began the workbook by considering the need to segregate client money from corporate assets:

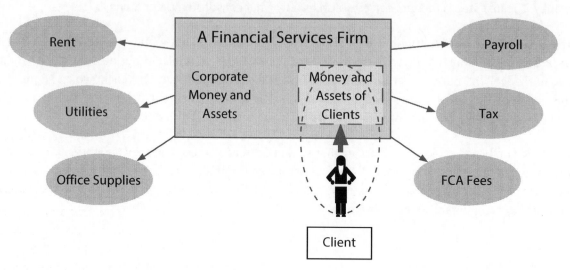

CASS 7 requires the firm to segregate the sums that are to be treated as client money. This is achieved by having distinct bank accounts, specifically:

- client bank accounts (CBAs) (containing money that the firm is treating as client money under the two broad categories described above), and
- corporate bank accounts (used for the firm's own commercial activity).

Let us now consider how a firm should handle the sums of money it receives from external parties, to ensure that appropriate segregation of client money is achieved. CASS 7 defines two approaches that a firm might use in order that the correct segregation is achieved.

2.1 'The Normal Approach' to Client Money Segregation

Learning Objective

3.1.1 Understand the normal approach to client money segregation

Under 'the normal approach' to segregation, the firm should first consider what types of transaction or interaction would result in an external party remitting money to the firm. It must then consider whether such sums being received would fit within the five legs of our abridged client money definition:

'Money…that a firm receives…from its client or for its client……in connection with designated investment business…unless a CASS 7 exemption is applied.'

For any sums that the firm considers would be client money when received, 'the normal approach' to segregation requires the firm to ensure that the external party will remit those monies directly into a client bank account of the firm and not first pay the money into a corporate account.

Let's consider some simple examples (ignoring at present the potential that the firm might be applying any CASS 7 exemptions). The firm produces an application form for its **designated investment business**, and includes its bank account details so that the investor can remit their investment sum. If the firm is operating under 'the normal approach' to segregation, the firm should ensure that the bank account details it provides are those of a client bank account rather than a corporate account.

If the firm offers the investor the choice of enclosing a cheque rather than remitting the money electronically, the firm should ensure that its operational processes are to pay that cheque directly in to the client bank account, rather than banking the money to the firm's corporate account and subsequently transferring it to the client bank account.

Similarly, the firm should ensure that other business relationships (ie, those relationships that are not related to its client-designated business) do not use the client bank account.

Note that the details of both the client bank account and the corporate account may become publicly known, and so it is possible that some remitting party will send money to the 'wrong' account. If such an error is made by the remitting party despite the firm providing the correct information, the firm has still complied with 'the normal approach', but must ensure that its downstream daily CASS controls can identify any such cases and promptly rectify the payer's error. If, however, the firm had incorrectly published its corporate bank account details rather than the client bank account details, resulting in money being remitted directly to the corporate account, such a situation would be viewed as breaching 'the normal approach'.

'The normal approach' to client money segregation should therefore ensure that any money the firm receives which ought to be segregated in a client bank account is segregated immediately. This act of segregation then enables all downstream CASS controls to be brought into effect. It should also be noted that 'the normal approach' requires that the firm segregate such receipts as client money even if it is not yet certain which client the monies relate to. We will return to this issue of 'allocating client money' later on.

The CASS rules enable some firms to adopt an alternative approach to segregation, and we will return to this 'alternative approach' in section 5 of this chapter.

3. Client Bank Accounts (CBAs)

Learning Objective

3.2.1 Know where, and into which types of account, client money can be deposited

3.2.2 Know the definitions of general client bank accounts and designated client bank accounts

The previous section made reference to client bank accounts (CBAs) – the bank accounts into which client money would be ultimately deposited under either approach referenced above. In this section, we will look at the characteristics and requirements of a CBA.

In chapter 1, we highlighted that effective protection of the client's assets needs the firm to successfully demonstrate both legal and physical segregation. Client money is segregated under the CASS rules through the use of a statutory trust, and the client bank account is key to achieving both the outcomes needed to achieve an effective trust structure.

The client bank account is a bank account that exists only to hold client money – which we have seen is made up of:

1. money the firm receives as part of its designated investment business, which satisfies the five-leg abridged definition, and
2. other money that the CASS rules specifically confirm must be treated as client money (which we will discuss in detail later).

We have just seen that 'normal approach to segregation' required this first type of client money to be received directly into the client bank account. Any other money that the firm recognises ought to be segregated because of specific CASS rules will similarly be segregated by the firm into the client bank account (generally transferring the money from its corporate bank account). This achieves physical segregation, and ensuring that no other corporate money remains in the client bank account is vital to ensuring that no pollution of trust arises.

However, physical segregation must be accompanied by legal segregation, and so establishing a client bank account is not simply a matter of the firm picking one of its bank accounts for this purpose. Both the firm and the bank must clearly differentiate the client bank account as legally existing for the purpose of segregating client money. Without this legal segregation, if the firm was to become insolvent the insolvency practitioner working to resolve the firm's affairs might be required to treat the contents of the client bank account as being a corporate asset, and use the money to settle the overall debts of the firm (rather than the money being secured for the firm's financial services clients).

In respect of the Client Money rules, the FCA Handbook defines a 'client bank account' as either:

*   a current account or deposit account at a bank, expressly held in the firm's name for the purposes of segregating client money, or
*   a money market deposit account, identified as being client money.

The definition then adds that in either case the account should be identified as:

*   a general client bank account
*   a designated client bank account, or
*   a designated client fund account.

We will now consider these aspects.

3.1   Where can a Client Bank Account be Opened?

The CASS rules require that firms place client money in an account opened with one of the following:

*   a central bank (as the central banks in some jurisdictions will enable accounts to be held)
*   a Capital Requirements Directive (CRD) credit institution (essentially now defined as a bank with its head office in the UK)

- a bank authorised in a third country (meaning a bank authorised outside the UK), or
- a qualifying money market fund (QMMF) – a type of authorised CIS which enables unitholders to readily sell their units and so receive cash promptly.

You will note that the first three of these options are all types of bank – and so satisfy the definition of "client bank account" noted above. While a firm can place client money within a QMMF, the QMMF does not however satisfy the definition of a 'client bank account'. You will also recall that 'the normal approach' to client money segregation required the firm to immediately segregate money into a client bank account. Therefore, while a firm may choose to use QMMFs as part of its overall client money arrangements, it is important to note that a QMMF itself falls outside of the defined term 'client bank account' and its use must be agreed to by the client.

As part of discussing broader controls over client money within chapter 4 of this workbook, we will explore the controls that a firm will have in place regarding the selection of an individual bank and the considerations of that choice.

3.2   What are these Three Types of Client Bank Account?

The definition of client bank account requires it to be identified as one of three types of account – each of which is defined in the Glossary of the FCA Handbook. The reason these three different types of CBA can exist is because of the flexibility offered by CASS which enables the firm to determine the best way to effect legal segregation within the context of its own financial services offering and the business model in operation. The following table considers the three options:

Term	Meaning
General Client Bank Account	As you would expect, this is the most general type of CBA. It holds money of the firm's clients in general. The name of the account must distinguish it from the firm's own money.
Designated Client Bank Account	An account used to hold the client money of only certain of the firm's clients, who have agreed in writing to their client money being held with the bank concerned. In technical terms, each designated client bank account creates a 'pool' of client money which is separate from any other CBA in operation (pooling will be discussed later in the book). The account name must include the words 'designated client'.
Designated Client Fund Account	An account used to hold at least part of the client money held for one or more clients, each of whom has consented to their money being held in such a CBA. If the bank holding a designated client fund account was to fail, each designated client fund account held by the firm with that bank would be brought together to form a single 'pool' (rather than each account forming a separate pool, as in the case of a designated client bank account).

Our focus in this chapter is about establishing the bank accounts necessary to support the firm's business model, and to understand how those accounts will deliver the legal and physical segregation required to ensure that the client money trust is operable, it is important to recognise that the firm will be allocating these sums of client money to individual clients within its own internal ledgers. We will explore the firm's records of client allocation in greater detail in chapter 4; the following sections consider what the CASS rules require in respect of actual movements of client money.

3.3   How is Legal Segregation Demonstrated?

Learning Objective

3.2.3   Know the function of an acknowledgement letter

3.2.4   Be able to apply the requirements of CASS to completing an acknowledgement letter, using the FCA templates

In order to ensure that money in a CBA will be successfully segregated, the trust status of the account must be acknowledged by the bank used. This is achieved through use of an 'acknowledgement letter': as described in CASS 7.18R.

An acknowledgement letter is a legal document, using wording specified in the CASS rules, which evidences the nature and purpose of the trust being established over the client money.

The CASS rules contain three different templates, each designed to achieve the same outcome but drafted to reflect the specific relationships the firm may form with different types of organisation. At this point we will focus upon the acknowledgement letter that is applied where money is being held with a bank – which is known in CASS as the Client Bank Account Acknowledgement Letter. Each template primarily comprises 'fixed text' (which must not be changed), with a small amount of 'variable text' (which the firm should complete or amend accordingly).

In order to ensure the trust is legally secure, the firm should apply the following approach:

1. Open the account with the relevant institution, ensuring that any relevant wording is included in the account name.
2. Select the correct acknowledgement letter template (here we will assume the client bank account acknowledgement letter).
3. The firm then completes the variable text, prints the letter on its own headed paper, and arranges for it to be signed by the relevant internal signatory.
4. The signed letter is then sent to the bank, who will countersign the letter and return it to the firm. Note: CASS requires the firm to use 'reasonable endeavours' to confirm that the person countersigning on behalf of the bank was authorised to do so – and retain evidence to this effect.
5. This provides the firm with documented evidence that both the bank and the firm have acknowledged that the money held in that account is legally segregated as relating to the firm's clients.

Importantly, in normal circumstances, the firm should not place any money into a new CBA until it has received the countersigned acknowledgement letter back from the bank, and ensured that the letter has been correctly completed. Remember – any error could put at risk any client money balance held within that CBA.

The firm should retain each acknowledgement letter (along with any other supporting documentation it considers relevant, including evidence that the countersignatory was authorised) until at least five years after it ceases to use the relevant account. It should also establish a periodic control (at least annually, per CASS) to ensure that it holds a completed, correct, and countersigned acknowledgement letter for each CBA in place.

The rules do recognise that in certain unusual circumstances the firm might need to change its CBA arrangements – such as transferring its banking arrangements to a different bank, or following the failure of a bank. While the first of these examples would be part of a substantial project within the firm, and the second example would potentially arise without the firm having much advance notice of the problem, the CASS rules recognise the potential that in such circumstances it might be impractical for the firm to obtain the countersigned copy of the acknowledgement letter prior to needing to apply client money to the new accounts opened. In such cases, CASS permits the firm to use the new CBAs for up to 20 business days after the firm sent the signed letter to the bank. However, if the countersigned copy is not received by the end of that 20-day period, the firm must cease using the affected accounts.

Note that this is an example where CASS accepts the potential of investor exposure, as the client money would be exposed to risk of loss until the countersigned acknowledgement letter has been received and validated. The CASS rules do not attempt to eliminate all risk of investor loss, but to reasonably minimise such potential for loss within the practical realities of interactions between different types of regulated institution.

3.4   Physical Receipts of Client Money

Learning Objective

3.2.5   Understand when money becomes client money, including the treatment of interest and commission

A firm can receive money in two broad ways. It can 'pull' money from the payer (such as when it banks a cheque, which results in the bank collecting the money and depositing it in the account chosen by the firm). Alternatively, money might be 'pushed' to the firm's bank account by the payer (such as where a BACS Payment Schemes Limited (BACS) transfer or telegraphic transfer is performed).

It follows that the firm's CASS obligations will be different in these two scenarios. Where the bank pulls money to itself, the firm is clearly responsible for ensuring that instructions are made according to the type of money being received (client money or corporate money) and whether the firm is applying 'the normal approach to client money segregation' (in which case, any client money being received should be received directly into a CBA).

The CASS rules include specific comment regarding physical receipts of client money – which might be actual cash but would also include cheques or payable orders received by the firm (as CASS considers such cheques to be 'money'). Therefore, if the firm is operating under the normal approach to client money segregation, the firm should deposit the cheque (or physical cash) into a CBA no later than the business day following receipt of that item by the firm. If the firm is operating under 'the alternative approach' to segregation, then the firm is obliged to bank the money to a corporate account within that same time frame. (We will return to 'the alternative approach' later in this chapter.)

In most cases, the firm will not unduly delay banking the money, though if the money does need to be retained by the firm rather than immediately banked, it must be held in a secure location. The firm should also record the receipt in the firm's books and records.

CASS does however recognise a scenario in which the money need not be paid into the bank account within this time frame. This is where some restriction of the regulatory system would effectively prevent the firm taking such action. An example of this would be where the firm has not been able to complete sanctions screening for a client it has received money from. If the firm was to bank the money, it may result in a breach of sanctions law and/or regulations.

Therefore, CASS permits a firm to determine whether some other regulatory obligation should override the need to bank any physical money received.

3.5   Amounts 'Due and Payable' to the Client (from the Firm)

The above sections have focused upon the need for the firm to recognise and process monies that are received into its bank accounts, to ensure that the correct segregation is achieved. However, we must also recognise that, at times, the firm will determine that certain sums of money are due to its client regardless of whether any actual money has been received by the firm. Such obligations will usually be documented within the terms and conditions that define the service being provided to the client. The most common scenario where money becomes due and payable from the firm to the client is where the firm has entered into a principal trade with the client, meaning that the firm must pay the client settlement proceeds when the client delivers the securities.

3.5.1   Contractual Settlement

For example, in chapter 1 we considered 'contractual settlement'. If a firm offers contractual settlement when selling the client's asset, it follows that the firm will consider the settlement proceeds are due and payable to the client with effect from the settlement date (regardless of whether the asset sale has actually completed in the financial markets).

In such a case, the firm will allocate money to the client because it has already determined its obligation to do so. If the firm will pay that allocated money to the client by close of business on the next day, the payment can be made directly from the firm's corporate bank account (as it is a sum 'due and payable from the firm to the client' as a result of the contractual arrangements between the parties). Otherwise, the firm must segregate the money to a client bank account in line with the allocation performed.

3.5.2 Bank Interest

Another example, slightly more complicated, is the treatment of bank interest earned on client bank accounts. CASS 7 requires that any interest earned on client money held for a client should be paid to that client – unless the firm has notified the client in writing that a different approach will be taken.

Consider the example where the firm operates a set of designated client bank accounts, such that each client's money is held in isolation. In such a context, it is a simple task to allocate whatever interest has been received to the client whose money makes up that account balance. While the interest will generally be accruing each day, the firm's terms and conditions are likely to state that the interest sum will only be due and payable to the client once it has been received from the bank.

Contrast this simple approach with the position if a firm is servicing a large number of retail clients within a single general client bank account. The interest received on that account is a result of potentially thousands of entries moving across the account during the month, and allocating that total interest so that each client receives the amount arising on their own personal activity becomes a difficult task. Where a firm does choose to effect an interest allocation (rather than notifying the clients that any such interest will be claimed instead by the firm), it is common for the firm to simply specify a rate of interest which it will pay, and to effect its own daily accrual based on its own ledger of client entitlement. Such an approach effectively results in the firm paying interest to its clients based upon its own accounting rather than on the sum received from the bank. The firm determines the amount that is 'due and payable' to each client, regardless of what interest is received.

3.5.3 Other Payments

Some firms will offer contractual arrangements under which the firm will pay sums of money (or other benefits) to the client. For example, the firm might offer to pay back a portion of a servicing charge if the client retains a balance above a certain level during the period. Such a rebate will become 'due and payable' to the client from the date at which the relevant contract stipulates that the commission amount should be recognised. CASS therefore requires contractual commission arrangements to be treated as client money from the date at which the contract states those sums become due and payable to the client. Similarly, once fee overpayments or compensation have been calculated they should be considered due and payable to the client.

It therefore follows that where a firm might choose to make a voluntary payment to the client – such as a condolence gift following a bereavement, or an *ex gratia* payment to apologise for a service failing – such sums are not related to any contractual obligation that the firm owes to its client. Such sums are not therefore 'due and payable' to the client as a result of the designated investment business being performed. Accordingly, such sums remain corporate expenses of the firm and are not items of client money governed by CASS. Of course, if the client pays that money back to the firm, or otherwise instructs the firm to use the money for investment purposes, at that point the firm would treat the money as a new client money receipt and ensure segregation and allocation of the money.

3.6 Releasing Money from Client Money Segregation

Learning Objective

3.2.6 Understand when money ceases to be client money

In the previous sections we have explored the types of activity that should result in the firm segregating money as client money – either because money has been received by the firm in connection with an investor's activity, or because the firm's contractual arrangements with the investor mean that a certain sum of money is now 'due and payable' to the investor. (Note: there are a range of exemptions that can relax this treatment, though these will be discussed later.)

We will now see what the CASS rules say about when the firm is permitted to remove client money from segregation. There are specific actions and circumstances in which the firm's obligations under the client money trust are deemed to have been satisfied; the legal term is that the firm has 'discharged its fiduciary duty'. The firm must prevent pollution of the trust, so it must ensure that having discharged any particular fiduciary duty it does not continue to segregate a corresponding sum as client money.

The following table outlines the situations in which CASS confirms that the firm has discharged its fiduciary duty. Before looking at the scenarios it is important to highlight that CASS does not specify that payments related to client money must be paid from the client bank account. Rather the rules enable a firm to make its own structural business decision as to whether to effect payments from a corporate bank account instead (and continue to segregate and allocate the relevant sum in a client bank account until the corporate payment has been successfully completed). The following scenarios therefore clarify the point at which the firm's fiduciary duty is discharged, and if any corresponding payment had been completed using a corporate account, the fact that fiduciary duty is discharged on that date enables the firm to release a corresponding sum from the client bank account back to the corporate account.

Scenario	Comment
Money is paid to the client or the client's representative	This relates to direct payments of cash to the client or their agent. (Note: payments to the client's personal bank account is regarded as a separate scenario in CASS.)
The firm pays the money to a third party on the client's instructions (or with their consent) to effect a transaction	We have seen that transactions require settlement on a specific date, and the third parties referenced by the CASS rules include entities such as an exchange, clearing house, or intermediate broker. CASS is clear that the firm should effect settlement payments necessary to conclude the investor's business – and that by effecting such a payment to a third party the firm has discharged its fiduciary duty. (Note that the discharge of fiduciary duty is not dependent upon the receipt of the corresponding asset; the discharge is effective because the payment is due.)

Scenario	Comment
The firm pays the money to a third party where necessary to satisfy an obligation on the firm related to the business being undertaken for the client	This is similar to the point above, but would include a wider range of payments. A firm must understand any payments that are necessary in order to effect the client's business, and if any fall into this category then the firm should ensure that its CASS treatment is correct.
The firm transfers the client's business to a different regulated firm	Each regulated firm is a business, and on occasion a firm may decide to stop offering certain services. At such times, the firm will usually arrange for another firm to take over providing those services, if the client so wishes, and the client's business is transferred to the new firm. CASS sets out the requirements by which any client money held by the original firm can be transferred over to the new firm, and the fiduciary duty of the first firm is discharged.

This scenario is specifically excluded from the 'third party' routes in the rows above because, in addition to consent or instruction from the client, the firm is required to assess whether the new firm has appropriate measures in place to protect client money.

(Note: there is a *de minimis* provision in CASS which confirms that if the balance being transferred for a retail client is less than £25, or less than £100 for other types of client, this extra '**due diligence**' requirement does not apply). |
| Money is paid into the bank account of the client | Rather than paying cash, the firm might effect a payment to the client's personal bank account (by BACS transfer, or sending a cheque). CASS states that this bank account cannot be in the firm's name, and must not be an account that the firm opened without the client's consent.

Note that, in respect of payments by cheque, CASS also clarifies that the discharge of fiduciary duty occurs when the sum is paid by the bank. If the cheque has been drawn on the CBA, this is automatically satisfied as the money remains segregated until the bank pays the presented cheque. If, however, the cheque is drawn on a corporate account, the firm should not assume that the cheque will be cashed on a specific date, and so should not release the corresponding sum of client money until the bank account statement shows that the money has been taken from the firm's bank account. |

Scenario	Comment
Money that is now due and payable to the firm	Certain events result in money that was previously client money effectively being used to settle a debt that the client owes to the firm. An obvious example would be where the firm's terms and conditions record a servicing fee or charge that will be applied to the client's account at regular intervals. Suppose for example that the firm levies an annual charge of £50 on 31 March each year for maintaining an account. Until 31 March, that sum is not due and payable to the firm, so it should remain allocated to the client and segregated as client money. However, on 31 March the firm is entitled to that money and so the £50 can be taken as corporate money in settlement of the debt now payable.
	Another example can arise depending on the mechanisms used by a firm to settle market transactions. Suppose the firm uses corporate money to place market purchase orders (while retaining the corresponding client money segregated in a CBA). Once the settlement date of the trade is reached, and the firm records the asset as having been bought, the firm could consider that the purchase price is now due and payable from client to firm.
Money identified in a reconciliation as an excess in the CBA	Daily client money reconciliations are an important control, and will be discussed in detail later in this workbook. As we will see then, where an internal reconciliation determines there to be an '**excess**', CASS requires that amount to be withdrawn from the segregated CBA in order to avoid pollution of the trust.
	Note that such money is not being declared 'due and payable' to the firm – there is no business or legal debt to be satisfied; the firm is simply obliged to remove the money because the reconciliation control determines the amount to be an excess.
Money paid by an authorised central counterparty directly to the client	Some services offered to a client would require a firm to place client money with an authorised central counterparty (CCP). Examples would include services enabling derivative transactions. If the firm then fails in its obligations (ie, the firm defaults), then the default management process of the authorised CCP can see the money paid directly to the clients concerned. Such payments are recognised as discharging the fiduciary duty originally owed by the firm.
Money paid by an authorised central counterparty to a clearing member (other than the firm) in connection with a porting arrangement	This also relates to corporate failure when client money has been placed with an authorised CCP. A porting arrangement enables the business arrangements of a failing clearing member to be moved to a different clearing member. Where this arises and the firm itself has failed, the porting event is viewed as a discharge of fiduciary duty in respect of the client money transferred.

Scenario	Comment
Money transferred by the firm to a clearing member in connection with a regulated clearing arrangement, then remitted to another firm/clearing member	Where the firm places money with a clearing member as part of a regulated clearing arrangement, a business failure may cause the clearing member to activate its default management procedures. Such movement from one clearing member to another is recognised as discharging the fiduciary duty of the firm.
Money transferred by the firm to a clearing member in connection with a regulated clearing arrangement, then remitted directly to the indirect clients of the firm	Similar to the above scenario, though here the money is distributed by the clearing member to the indirect clients of the firm. Again, this is seen as discharging the fiduciary duty of the firm to its clients.
Allocated but unclaimed client money paid away to charity (without a specific instruction from the client concerned)	Over time, a firm might find a balance of money arising for a given client – such as if the client does not bank the cheques received from the firm. Such balances need to remain allocated to the client concerned. CASS sets out a process by which a firm can discharge its fiduciary duty for such allocated balances, and so is no longer required to hold that money as client money. This process enables the firm to pay such monies to a chosen charity, without receiving an instruction from the client to do so. The process is set out in more detail below.

3.7 Payment to Charity of Allocated but Unclaimed Client Money

Learning Objective

3.2.7 Know the treatment of allocated but unclaimed client money

As noted in the table above, on occasion a firm will find itself unable to effect payment back to its client. This is most commonly because the client has failed to bank a cheque, often combined with the news that the client has changed address (as firms do not wish to enable fraudulent activity by sending further correspondence to a client who has 'gone away' from their last known residential address).

CASS enables a firm to pay to a registered charity sums of allocated but unclaimed client money, providing the client's balance has been held by the firm for at least six years (ie, the only transactions passing on the account are not customer-directed and relate to periodic events, such as interest or fees).

Where the balance is small (less than £25 for a retail client, and less than £100 for other types of client) the firm need only make one fresh attempt to contact the client at the last known address and so attempt to repay the money. If the client has not responded after 28 days, the firm can affect the payment to the nominated charity and so discharge its fiduciary duty in respect of that sum. The firm must maintain records of the balances paid away by this method, including the respective client and the charity receiving the money.

Where the balance is larger (over £25 for a retail client, or over £100 for other types of client) the process is more complex, as CASS sets out a more prescriptive set of 'reasonable steps' that the firm should perform to attempt to reunite the client with their money, shown below:

1. Determine as far as reasonably possible that the contact details held by the firm are correct.
2. Write to the client at the last known address (either post or electronic mail) advising that the balance on account will be paid to charity if the client does not respond within 28 days.
3. After those 28 days, the firm must then attempt a further communication via a different channel. (The CASS rules suggest telephone calls or media advertisements might be considered.) This communication will again warn that after 28 days the money will be paid away to charity.
4. If the client has still not contacted the firm once those 28 days have elapsed, one further written communication should be made (either via post or electronic mail) to confirm that in 28 days' time the money will be paid to charity – though also noting that the firm will remain obliged to pay the client an equivalent sum if they make contact with the firm in the future.
5. Once that final set of 28 days has elapsed, the firm may pay the balance to charity and discharge its fiduciary duty.

CASS confirms that if the firm has received confirmation that the contact details it holds for the client are no longer correct (eg, it knows the client to be 'gone away' from their last known address), it need not send communications to those contact details. However, 'reasonable steps' would still need to be demonstrated, and so some firms may consider the use of tracing services before effecting the payment to charity.

Note that for these larger sums, the firm remains legally obliged to effect payment to the client in the future – despite the client money having been paid to charity and the firm's fiduciary duty having been discharged. In such cases, the firm may benefit from a simplified operational process once the stale balances are removed – but does so only by incurring a potential future financial liability. The firm or a member of its group must, before paying away such balances, make an unconditional undertaking that it will pay the equivalent sum to any client making a later valid claim. This undertaking must be authorised by the firm's governing body, be legally enforceable and must be retained indefinitely.

Full and detailed records must therefore be kept when any firm chooses to pay allocated but unclaimed client money away to a charity without an instruction from the client.

The CASS rules also require that any costs incurred by the firm in satisfying these requirements to pay allocated but unpaid money away to a charity must be borne by the firm and not passed on to the client. Such costs include both the operational costs of trying to contact the client, but also the cost of any insurance retained by the firm against potential future claims.

3.8   Mixed Remittance

Learning Objective

3.2.8   Know how to treat mixed remittance

It is possible that a given client might make a payment to a firm that is intended to serve multiple purposes. For example, suppose the client owes a sum of money to the firm (such as an outstanding fee for the firm's services), but also wishes to make a further investment in assets (being effected by the firm as part of that service). By definition, the money being paid to the firm to settle an outstanding debt is not client money, as the money is already due and payable to the firm as a creditor of the client. However, the additional money destined for investment purposes should be treated as client money.

CASS rules describe such a payment as a 'mixed remittance', ie, a single receipt which includes money that is client money as well as money that is corporate money of the firm.

Where the firm is using the normal approach to segregation, CASS requires the firm to receive the full sum into a client bank account. The firm would then process the money through its ledgers and determine the portion that is due and payable to the firm. Once the firm believes the amount has been 'cleared' by the bank (ie, the money is actually available to withdraw), the portion identified as being due and payable to the firm would then be removed from segregation.

3.9   Use of Multiple Currencies

Learning Objective

3.2.9   Know the requirements around client money held in different currencies

Financial services is an international industry, and many firms will offer services to their clients enabling them to invest in assets domiciled in a range of countries. As such, firms will need to manage the consequences of handling client money in multiple currencies.

Again, CASS does allow firms some freedom in how to arrange these facilities. It would be possible for the firm to at all times retain client money in sterling, providing it ensures that this approach is in line with the terms and conditions defining the services being provided.

However, in some cases, there will be client money arising in multiple currencies – either in order to effect market settlement of asset transactions, or when receiving dividends or other payments arising from assets held. In such cases, it would be possible for the firm to open CBAs in the relevant currency – providing the bank concerned provides the completed acknowledgement letter.

As this might not be possible, CASS also allows a third option. The firm is allowed to hold the client money in a different currency from the actual currency in which the money was received or is due to the client. However, if the firm uses this approach it must perform a daily calculation to ensure that the amount segregated (in the chosen currency) is at least equal to the value due to the client. This conversion calculation must be performed daily based on the close of business exchange rates on the prior day.

Where the firm opens a CBA in a non-sterling currency, all other CBA-related controls are applicable to that CBA.

4. Client Transaction Accounts (CTAs)

Learning Objective

3.3.1 Know the difference between client bank accounts and client transaction accounts and the different treatments of each

In this chapter we have focused on the need for the firm to segregate client money in a CBA, the need to ensure a legal trust is in place over that money (achieved by completing the relevant acknowledgement letter), and ensuring that the firm knows when its fiduciary duty is discharged.

There is, however, an additional type of account that may also be relevant to the segregation of client money, depending on the types of services that a firm offers. This type of account is called a **client transaction account (CTA).** While a CTA will only be required by a fraction of the firms that handle client money, it is important to understand how CBAs and CTAs differ in order to understand the application of the client money controls that will be discussed in the next chapter.

While a CBA is opened at a bank, enabling the firm to deposit sums of client money to ensure ongoing segregation, a CTA is opened with a third party through which the firm intends to perform transactions for its clients and should only be used for money directly required to effect a transaction with or through that third party.

One example quoted in the CASS rules is the scenario where a firm transfers client money to a clearing house to act as a margin payment for a transaction being undertaken, but a CTA may also be applicable if the firm was transacting business through an exchange, intermediate broker, or a counterparty used by the firm in conducting 'over-the-counter' derivative activity.

While a CTA should only be used to hold client money necessary to complete a client order/transaction (rather than to hold general balances of segregated client money) it is still necessary to secure a CTA by obtaining an acknowledgement letter. The wording of that acknowledgement letter is however different (being the standardised template wording found in CASS 7). It is therefore important for the firm to ensure that it understands the type of acknowledgement letter that the third party will complete, and to use the correct template wording. As with the other forms of acknowledgement letter, the third party should countersign the letter and return it to the firm.

Another way in which a firm might use a CTA is in respect of assets held for its clients. CASS requires that where safe custody assets are deposited with a third party (we will discuss such arrangements when discussing custody later in the workbook), the firm must ensure that the third party takes one of the following approaches in respect of any client money arising on those assets:

1. Directly pay such money into a client bank account of the firm. (Note: if the third party is itself a bank, this might be achieved by the third party operating a CBA for the firm.)
2. Record such monies in a client transaction account for the benefit of the firm's clients.

Such monies may include dividends or other income received on the assets, or the proceeds of asset sale transactions.

The following table highlights the two key differences between CBAs and CTAs, as noted in CASS 7:

Client Bank Account	Client Transaction Account
Can only be opened with a bank	Can be opened at any third party (other than a bank) with which the firm is transacting
Can be used to hold sums of segregated client money on deposit	Should not be used to maintain balances of client money, but should only contain the monies required for transactions being undertaken

The full wording of the different acknowledgement letter templates can be seen in CASS 7, and many of the clauses in the CBA acknowledgement letter also appear in the CTA acknowledgement letter. However, it is interesting to see some of the ways in which the two templates differ. Remember that in each case, the letter should be written by the firm on its headed paper and countersigned by the bank/third party to demonstrate their agreement to the terms contained.

The CBA template states:

> 'we hold all money standing to the credit of the client bank account in our capacity as trustee under the laws applicable to us'.

The corresponding paragraph of the CTA template states to the third party:

> 'you are instructed to promptly credit to this client transaction account any money you receive in respect of any transaction that we have notified to you as being carried out on behalf of our clients'.

Note how these two clauses set the operational expectations for how these different accounts will function. Correct use of a CTA is dependent upon the firm clearly identifying for the third party whether a given transaction is being carried out for its clients – such that the third party must then process movements in line with the instruction documented in the acknowledgement letter. By contrast, the CBA letter simply confirms to the bank that the firm is acting as trustee in respect of money held in the CBA.

The CBA template includes some wording not found in the CTA template, requiring the bank to release on demand by the firm (or any liquidator, receiver, administrator or trustee appointed over the firm's affairs) any money held in the CBA. The letter does confirm that in such a case the bank would be entitled to retain any sums due to the bank as agreed fees for running the CBA (though the bank could not use money from a CBA to settle any debt owed by the firm in respect of other accounts operated). It is important to note that the bank does not have any right of set-off or lien in respect of CBAs, ie, it is not able to use money from a CBA to pay off a debt relating to another account it maintains for the firm.

The CBA template also includes a clear statement by the firm that the bank is not responsible for ensuring that the firm complies with its obligations as trustee for the CBA.

The CTA template similarly has some wording not found in the CBA template. The CTA acknowledgement letter confirms that all money credited to the CTA will be payable to the firm in its role as trustee – except where default by the firm means that the third party applies its default management process and so transfers the money to another party (in the ways noted earlier as constituting a discharge of the firm's fiduciary duty).

5. 'The Alternative Approach' to Client Money Segregation

Learning Objective

3.4.1   Understand the alternative approach to client money segregation and the approaches to managing risk arising from its use

In this chapter, we have so far considered 'the normal approach' to client money segregation, by which client money is immediately segregated upon receipt. (Note: there are some exemptions that can be applied, and we will explore those later in section 7.) CASS 7 recognises that in some circumstances applying this 'normal approach' could itself result in excessive operational risk – which could undermine the consumer protection that the client money rules are intended to provide. CASS 7, therefore, permits a firm to adopt an alternative arrangement – helpfully called 'the alternative approach' – which the firm might apply to specific business lines according to the relevant context and operational risk.

Under the alternative approach to segregation, the firm will receive client money into a corporate account, while performing a daily calculation to determine how much money the firm should ensure is segregated as client money for the protection of its clients. The result of this is best demonstrated by considering what would happen if a client was to make a payment to the firm today – and to assume that no other movements occur on this day.

Suppose the payment is £10,000. A firm using 'the normal approach' would receive that money directly into its CBA. At the end of today the amount segregated would be £10,000 higher than the balance at close of business yesterday. However, if the firm had used 'the alternative approach' to segregation, the closing balance today would remain unchanged. Tomorrow the firm will perform its daily calculation to determine how much money ought to be segregated as of close of business today, and will therefore segregate the £10,000 sum tomorrow as part of its daily control processes.

As you can see, 'the alternative approach' therefore contains a built-in time lag; it runs one day behind the figures that would arise under 'the normal approach' (as the same pattern emerges for payments back to the client). This creates a potential risk, as the amount of client money that the firm may owe to its client population on any given day may be less than the amount actually segregated in the firm's CBAs.

To mitigate this risk, the rules enabling 'the alternative approach' require the firm to calculate an additional sum of money that it reasonably considers would have been sufficient to cover any such **shortfall** during the previous three months of business. The rules describe this figure as the 'alternative approach mandatory prudent segregation' figure, and the firm must add this value to the balance maintained in its CBAs. The firm must keep records to justify this calculation. (Note: this figure is different from any other '**prudent segregation**' that the firm may put in place, which is discussed in more detail in the next chapter.)

Due to the additional calculations and accounting complexity required to successfully apply the alternative approach, any firm wishing to use this approach for any of its business lines must first obtain a written report from an independent auditor to confirm that in the auditor's opinion the firm's systems and controls are suitably designed to deliver the alternative approach in line with CASS 7 requirements. This opinion includes the calculation of the alternative approach mandatory prudent segregation amount.

This process therefore takes time, and CASS requires that at least three months before it intends to apply the alternative approach, the firm must notify the FCA of its intention, and agree to make available any documentation requested by the FCA. Once the auditor's written report is received, the firm must send a copy to the FCA, again before it begins to apply the alternative approach. Principle 10 remains applicable to the firm, regardless of the segregation approach operated.

6. Other Money Segregated as Client Money

6.1 Unidentified and Unallocated Client Money

Learning Objective

3.5.1 Know the rules around allocation of client money, including unidentified and unallocated amounts

So far in this chapter we have looked at money that the firm has received from a specific client – such as by cash or cheque. However, the firm may receive client money in other ways too – such as where the client pays by a regular direct debit, arranged by the firm with the client's bank.

In all such cases, the firm is in some way in control of the money arriving at the bank; it can coordinate its records against the knowledge that the money is expected. As such, the firm should 'allocate' the money against the relevant client, making a clear record in the firm's systems that a given amount was received for/from a given client. These allocations are very important in ensuring that all client money is accurately accounted for, and that none is mislaid.

However, it is also possible for money to arrive when the firm is not expecting it, or for money to be 'pushed' to the firm's bank account rather than the firm 'pulling' the money from the client. For example, suppose the firm permits its clients to send money by telegraphic transfer or online banking instructions, such that the money will simply arrive within the firm's bank account accompanied only by whatever reference information has been passed on by the client's bank.

CASS places certain obligations on the firm to ensure that any such monies are also suitably protected. Firstly, if the firm is operating under 'the normal approach' to segregation, it should only provide clients with the bank details for the client bank account (rather than any corporate account of the firm). In this way, any client money that is received unexpectedly will be immediately segregated.

CASS also requires the firm to promptly investigate any such unexpected sums received, as such sums might be client money, or could actually be money that belongs to the firm. CASS uses the term 'unidentified client money' to describe such money, and unidentified monies should remain segregated as client money while the firm continues its efforts to determine whether the money is due to the company or is in fact client money. If the firm determines the money is client money, though remains unaware of the specific client(s) concerned, it should make a record in its systems to state that the relevant sum is 'unallocated client money'. If, however, the firm's investigations confirm that the money is actually corporate money rather than client money, it must at that time remove the money from the CBA.

Note that no retrospective CASS breach arises for any period for which a firm segregates such money as 'unidentified client money' (even if the money is later concluded to be corporate money). Often the investigations of 'unidentified' items will also confirm the relevant client, in which case the money should become allocated to the client in the usual way (rather than being recorded as 'unallocated'). It is possible, however, that on occasion the firm may be unable to identify the client responsible for sending the money, or conclude that the money might have been incorrectly sent to the firm. In such cases, CASS confirms that the firm would be justified in returning the money to the remitting party.

You will note in the above comments how important it is for the firm to maintain a complete and accurate record of client money allocation. CASS confirms that such allocation should be made 'promptly', though it does allow a firm up to ten business days following receipt to complete recording this allocation. (Note, however, that such a slow process could have business consequences – such as if a delay in allocation resulted in the client's transaction being delayed.)

If the allocation will not be achieved promptly (generally considered to be on the day of receipt, or potentially on the following day if the money arrives late in the afternoon) the firm must record the money as 'unallocated client money' to ensure that it can be fully accounted for within the reconciliation of client money (which will be discussed in the next chapter.)

As one example, a delay in allocation might arise if the sum of money received is an aggregated amount that needs to be shared out between many affected clients – such as a compensation amount received, or the disaggregation of a dividend. Firms must ensure that their records record the nature of all client money – whether allocated, unallocated, or unidentified.

6.2 Prudent Segregation

Learning Objective

On completion, the candidate should:

3.5.2 Understand the concept of prudent segregation

3.5.3 Know the record-keeping requirements around prudent segregation

Within any operational process, there is always the potential that errors or other scenarios may occur – whether within a firm, or in other parties along a transaction chain. Some scenarios could, in the firm's view, expose its clients to the risk that (in the event of the firm becoming insolvent before the matter is resolved) the total amount of segregated client money would be insufficient to pay each client the correct sum due.

For this reason, the CASS rules include a mechanism that enables a firm to protect its clients against this type of risk. This mechanism is known as prudent segregation, and permits a firm to place corporate money into a CBA in order to mitigate a specific risk identified and quantified by the firm. It may be used only when the firm considers this a reasonable means of protecting the clients against the identified risks. Importantly, prudent segregation amounts are never allocated to clients, and neither would the money be recorded as either 'unidentified' or 'unallocated' sums (as the money is not *due and payable from the firm to the client*, and neither has any client money been received by the firm for its clients).

In order that such amounts do not pollute the client money trust, any firm that intends to make use of prudent segregation must maintain certain documentation and record prudent segregation money movements in a particular way.

Firstly, the firm must prepare a policy document stating the risks for which that firm considers prudent segregation would become applicable. This policy document must be approved by the firm's governing body before any prudent segregation is put in place. The policy should also explain why the firm considers prudent segregation is a reasonable means of mitigating specific anticipated risks relating to the circumstances identified, and clarify how the firm will calculate the amount of money to be segregated in respect of each type of risk identified.

When any of the circumstances recorded in a firm's policy occur, prudent segregation will be put in place. Each cash movement of prudent segregation (whether into the CBA or out from the CBA) must be recorded, and the firm must create a specific record (known in CASS as a 'prudent segregation record') that clearly identifies the nature of the money and the purpose for the movement – which evidences that placing such corporate money into the CBA was not a pollution of the trust.

For any increase or decrease in the amount of prudent segregation in place, the prudent segregation record would include:

- the outcome of the calculation of the prudent segregation amount
- the amount paid into or withdrawn from the CBA
- why the payment or withdrawal was made
- confirmation that either:
    a. the payment was made in accordance with the firm's existing policy, or
    b. that the firm's policy will be amended in light of the circumstances
- confirmation that the payment or withdrawal has been made in accordance with the relevant rules, and
- a current total of prudent segregation money.

can be outside policy if necessary (handwritten annotation)

Different firms will therefore apply prudent segregation in respect of different types of potential risk exposures – in accordance with their own internal risk assessments and the policy they have written as a result. The firm will need to explain its policy to external parties, such as its auditor.

While each firm will make its own decision as to when prudent segregation money should be applied, one example scenario might run as follows. Note that this is a complex example, in order to draw out the various considerations that a firm will need to consider when deciding its approach to prudent segregation.

Date	Action/Comment
Monday 30 March	The firm receives instructions from a large number of clients, all wanting to buy units in a particular CIS.
31 March	The CIS has its annual accounting date, which triggers the calculation and subsequent payment of an income distribution to all registered holders of units.
2 April	The firm's settlements team recognises that the transaction to buy units in that CIS has not been settled. Investigation confirms that the firm failed to place an aggregated purchase of units on 30 March. As such, the firm has two problems: • It needs to buy the missing units – and ensure that any loss arising from the CIS unit price changing since 30 March is incurred by the firm rather than its clients. • The firm will not receive as much income distribution as it should have – because the firm held insufficient units as at the 31 March accounting reference date of the CIS.
3 April	The firm's initial investigations confirm that 5,389 of its clients had instructed the purchase of units in that CIS on 30 March, and the firm completes a calculation of the number of units that should have been purchased on 30 March. The firm instructs that purchase today at the next calculated price. A trade confirmation received later in the day confirms the actual price of the executed deal.
Monday 6 April	The firm can calculate the total loss made because of its error, ready for settlement on 8 April.

Date	Action/Comment
8 April	The trade settles and each investor receives the correct allocation of units.
Approx. 31 May	The CIS pays the distribution, so the firm receives a payment based on the number of units actually held as at 31 March. The firm must then calculate the amount of extra income it owes to its clients as a result of failing to purchase units on 30 March.

Importantly, while the firm will swiftly determine the effective timeline for correcting such an error, some necessary pieces of information cannot be known until later in the process. For example, the firm will not know the amount of income being distributed for each unit of the CIS until the end of May but it knows in early April that there will be some outstanding gap, ie, the client money pool is exposed to a potential deficit and the firm can at best only estimate the likely quantum of such an exposure.

This is a good example of where prudent segregation might be considered. The firm could use prior fund performance figures to estimate the likely income payment due for the aggregated market order that it failed to place on 30 March. It need not allocate such money to underlying clients – adding such estimated data into the client allocation records risks causing further confusion. However, the firm could place its own money into the CBA as prudent segregation ahead of the actual figures becoming known and the relevant allocations being made at client level. *just sensible.*

The firm might also consider whether prudent segregation would be applicable while correcting the missed deals themselves, and the firm's decision will be affected by two particular variables (and possibly others as well), namely:

- how the firm settles aggregated asset purchase deals, ie, from its corporate account or from a CBA, and
- how long the firm believes it will take to post the relevant corrective items against 5,389 client accounts.

If the firm's organisational structure is to settle market purchases from its corporate bank account (and discharge its fiduciary duty on settlement date by declaring the corresponding sums 'due and payable' to the firm) then it may proceed by settling the full market amount from its corporate account and only debiting client accounts with the cash value of their original transactions. In such a case, all asset purchases carry a risk that if the firm was to become insolvent prior to market settlement date, the investors could incur loss arising from failed settlement. *not enough in CBA.*

Alternatively, if the firm settles asset purchases from a client bank account, the firm will need to provide additional money to enable the settlement on 8 April because of the loss incurred. One approach is for the firm to effectively allocate to each client the money needed to complete their portion of the market transaction – in which case that extra money becomes 'due and payable' to the client and should be allocated. Until such allocation is completed, the risk remains.

It is therefore also important that such a firm considers how long it may take to post such underlying entries and allocate the relevant sums to each client. Where the allocation could take an extended period, the firm might again consider that prudent segregation should be put in place – securing the overall asset settlement while continuing to progress the allocations of specific sums for each client.

This one example should hopefully illustrate why each firm needs to give detailed and informed consideration to the scenarios that could give rise to risk for their clients – in the context of that firm's systems and processes – and why each firm may have a bespoke prudent segregation policy.

7. Exemptions

Learning Objective

3.6.1   Understand the use of exemptions available within the client money rules

---

7.1   Professional Client Opt-Out

Many regulations and controls function by reducing the potential scope of a firm's activity. In some cases, this is achieved by specifically prohibiting certain activities, or excluding certain types of assets. In other cases, the regulatory obligations simply make it uneconomical for a firm to undertake certain types of non-core business due to the costs of establishing the necessary controls.

However, the rules, at times, recognise that such restrictions can limit the overall flow of investments and money within the financial services market. In order to give some flexibility, the CASS 7 rules do allow a professional client to confirm that it wishes to opt out of CASS 7 protection, though only for non-MiFID business. This choice can only be taken in certain circumstances, and the professional client must recognise that, as a consequence, it will bear a greater potential loss in the event of the firm's insolvency. However, agreeing to use the opt-out might be the only way in which the firm and the professional client can reach a contractual agreement for the firm to undertake certain actions for that client.

The specific details of the professional client opt-out will be discussed in chapter 9.

7.2   Managers of Regulated Collective Investment Schemes (CISs)

In general, the managers of regulated CISs deal as principal when selling units to a client (or repurchasing those units from the client). In such a context, the firm makes a contract with its client to deal those units (that contract being subject to client money rules, with the settlement money being 'due and payable' between the firm and the client). Separately, due to its obligations under the Collective Investment Schemes (COLL) rules, the fund manager might instruct for the trustee to issue or cancel units (those transactions being corporate obligations).

CASS provides an exemption to the fund managers of regulated CISs. For payments from the firm to its client, the exemption simply echoes the usual CASS obligation for money 'due and payable from the firm'. The most important operational aspect of the exemption arises in respect of money being received from the client, as it allows the fund manager to receive that money into its corporate account without breaching 'the normal approach to segregation'. If the client's money is received by the fund manager more than one day prior to the contractual settlement date of a unit transaction, the firm must still segregate the money in a CBA (having first received it into a corporate account). If, however, the money is only received on the day prior to contractual settlement (or any subsequent day) then the fund manager need not move that money into a CBA.

In this way, unless the firm's client pays settlement monies more than one day before the contractual settlement date, the fund manager would not need to segregate the money as client money, though would still be viewed by the CASS rules as satisfying 'the normal approach'.

When making a payment following a repurchase of units, the fund manager must ensure that the cash settlement is completed by the day following the sum being due and payable to the investor (ie, the contractual settlement date of the client's transaction) or must segregate the money in a CBA. (Note that this reflects the usual expectations of 'the normal approach' to segregation in respect of money 'due and payable' from firm to client, as noted earlier.)

If a CIS's constitution established a model by which the money would be paid by the AFM to the trustee in advance of the contractual settlement date, the AFM could apply this DvP exemption – though would need to segregate and allocate as client money any sums that were not paid to the trustee concerned by close of business on the day following receipt.

7.3   Delivery versus Payment (DvP) Transactions

Where a firm is executing a delivery versus payment (DvP) transaction on behalf of a client, and does so using a 'commercial settlement system', a CASS exemption can be applied. However, the mechanics and operation of this exemption relate to an interaction between the firm's cash activity and its safe custody asset positions. As such, this particular CASS exemption will be discussed in chapter 5, section 3.4 (when both aspects of the exemption can be considered).

End of Chapter Questions

Think of an answer for each question and refer to the appropriate section for confirmation.

1. When an external party remits something of value to a firm, what five factors would determine whether the firm would treat it as client money? *Money, that a firm receives from a client, in connection w/ investments unless exemption applied*
   Answer reference: Section 1

2. What is 'the normal approach' to client money segregation, and how would it affect the firm's receipts processes? *straight into CBA* *→ must grade receipts is client money ever; not give what about*
   Answer reference: Section 2.1

3. As well as being able to hold client money in a qualifying money market fund (QMMF), what are the three types of institution at which a firm can hold client money? *Cbank, UK bank, foreign bank.*
   Answer reference: Section 3.1

4. How is legal segregation of client money achieved? *acknowledgement letter*
   Answer reference: Section 3.3

5. In what circumstances may money be 'due and payable to the client' from the firm? *contractual settlement, interest*
   Answer reference: Section 3.5

6. What is 'discharge of fiduciary duty', why is it important, and when does it occur? *firms obligatory satisfied = remove money from segregation.*
   Answer reference: Section 3.6

7. In terms of CASS 7, what is a 'mixed remittance' and how should it be treated? *corp money + client money - accounts.*
   Answer reference: Section 3.8

8. What is a client transaction account, where would it be opened and how would one be used?
   Answer reference: Section 4

9. What is the alternative approach to client money segregation? *Into corp account, then worked out how much set aside*
   Answer reference: Section 5

10. What risk is introduced by the alternative approach of client money segregation, and how is that risk addressed? *Time lag - alternative approach explanatory prudent segregation.*
    Answer reference: Section 5

11. What does CASS 7 mean by 'unidentified client money'? *unexpected amount received*
    Answer reference: Section 6.1

12. What information should be contained in the firm's prudent segregation record? *amount of calc, into/out CBA, why, longing date Config of policy or how pol will be updated, config of rules correct total.*
    Answer reference: Section 6.2

Chapter Four
Controls over Client Money (CASS 7)

This syllabus area will provide approximately 6 of the 50 examination questions

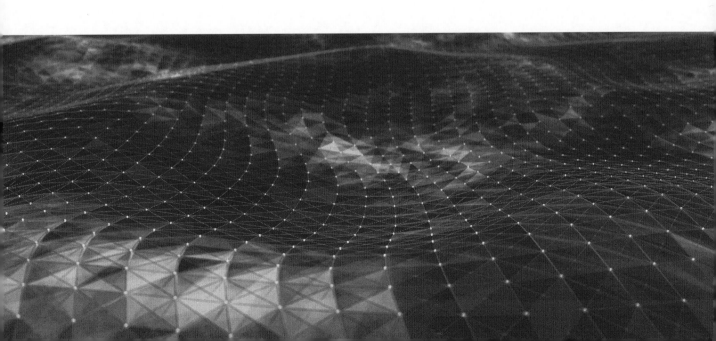

Introduction

In chapter 3 we discussed how client money is identified, and the ways in which a firm should segregate it – including the structure of client bank accounts (CBAs) and client transaction accounts (CTAs), understanding when a given sum of money should be segregated as client money, and the different types of event by which a firm can discharge its fiduciary duty and so end its responsibility to segregate that money.

In this chapter, we will look at a range of controls that CASS 7 requires a firm to establish and perform as part of ensuring that the client money arrangements are operating correctly. As we will see, these controls include detective measures to ensure that the firm is maintaining complete ledger records of cash movements, and that any shortfall in the level of client money held will be addressed on the day after it arises. Again, a firm should not rely just upon such daily controls in order to solve all potential issues; it must maintain adequate organisational arrangements to minimise the risk of client money being lost. However, this question of 'adequacy' remains a matter of judgement for the firm – and must be clearly explained to its auditor to ensure joint understanding.

It should also be noted that the controls discussed in this chapter are those specified by CASS. All firms will establish a wider control environment which is complementary to the CASS-specific controls and the types of business they undertake. It is important that each firm blends CASS controls into its overall business model.

1.   Controls over the Selection of a Bank

Learning Objective

4.1.1   Understand firms' responsibilities in respect of bank selection, appointment, and review

CASS 7 considers a central bank to be reliable. However, if the firm deposits client money with any other type of bank (such as a domestic high street banking group) the firm must exercise due skill, care and diligence in the selection and appointment of that bank. Such 'due diligence' will include the firm considering the bank's expertise and market reputation, together with reviewing any legal requirements or market practices that would impact the ways in which client money would be handled. Similar due diligence reviews should be performed on any Capital Requirements Directives (CRD) credit institution or qualifying money market fund (QMMF) used to hold client money.

Guidance in CASS 7 recommends that a firm consider the following when performing due diligence on a bank:

- the capital and credit-worthiness of the bank/QMMF (ie, does it look financially strong?)
- the proportion of the bank's total deposits that the firm's client money would represent (ie, would the firm's client money represent too high a proportion of the bank's balance sheet exposure?)

- for money to be held outside the UK, whether that money would be protected by any form of deposit protection scheme in that jurisdiction (ie, is there an equivalent to the UK's Financial Services Compensation Scheme (FSCS) – and, if so, how does that scheme function?)
- where possible, the level of risk accepted by the bank/third party in its investment and loan activities.

With memories of the global 'credit crunch' and subsequent banking crisis starting to fade, it is critical that the above factors are satisfied for UK banks or other regulated entities. However, we must remember that the CASS rules remain relevant to a UK firm when conducting international trade, and so any foreign bank accounts in other jurisdictions should also provide adequate protection of client money.

It follows that, if a firm does not consider that it can find a suitable bank/third party to provide services in a given jurisdiction, the firm might conclude that it cannot hold client money within that jurisdiction. The firm may therefore use local corporate accounts to support business interactions (providing all such interactions do not contravene specific CASS rules), while ensuring that adequate segregation is achieved using domestic CBAs.

In addition to all the above factors, if the firm is seeking to use a QMMF to hold client money, the firm should check whether there would be any restrictions on the amount and frequency of redemptions – to ensure that using the QMMF will not cause operational tension in effecting payments at the relevant time.

Once the firm is satisfied from this due diligence review that the bank/third party is appropriate (and remembering to perform all such due diligence on the specific legal entity with which the firm intends to contract, rather than looking only at a global group level), it can commence operations with that institution, subject to first fulfilling the acknowledgment letter requirements. The firm should periodically review its due diligence on that institution to ensure that no updated information would undermine its view of that institution. CASS does not specify a timescale for such reviews, and so the firm will determine a relevant frequency in the light of relevant factors (such as the jurisdiction concerned, the stability of economic conditions, and any pertinent market information and news).

1.1 How Many Banks Should a Firm Use?

Learning Objective

4.1.2 Understand the client money diversification rules

In normal circumstances, we all expect a bank to be stable – in which case a firm can be confident that money placed with a bank will be available when called upon. However, if a firm places all its client money in a single entity, any problem experienced by that entity (including system problems that prevent payments from being processed) would have a significant impact on the firm's business and obligations.

It therefore follows that each firm must consider the risks of holding all client money with a single entity and whether using two or more would be a more appropriate strategy. Such a decision requires consideration of a balance between risk reduction, operational complexity, business costs, and regulatory obligations – so let's start with the regulatory aspects.

CASS uses the term 'diversification' to describe this approach of splitting up the total client money balance between multiple banks, though CASS only requires a firm to 'diversify' its client money where the firm is using a bank or third party from within its own corporate group. The CASS requirement is that no more than 20% of the total client money held by the firm in its CBAs at any time can be held in CBAs run by relevant group entities.

To put this into context, most UK banking groups include an investment management division, such as a legal entity that manages collective investment schemes (CISs) or advisory and discretionary portfolios. Let's imagine XYZ Bank as an example. CASS allows the XYZ Fund Management company to have CBAs with XYZ Bank – but not more than 20% of the current total balance can be held in CBAs with XYZ Bank. Other CBAs would be required with banks outside the XYZ Group.

There are various operational means that might be considered in complying with this rule, and so each firm will need to determine which approach will best fit with its business model – which might simply be to only use external banks and so avoid the problem.

While a firm that does not use a group entity to hold CBAs is not therefore subject to this direct 20% limit, all firms are required by CASS to consider whether diversification should be part of their overall controls of client money. As noted above, while there can be a risk reduction aspect to diversification, the consequences for operational complexity can be significant – particularly for firms managing a high volume of transactions.

However, the FCA recognises the potential that this blanket 20% rule might be disproportionate for some firms. Therefore, if a firm only has small client money balances, has a business that is not unduly complex, and where the group entity concerned is considered to be safe given the information available, then the 20% limit can be set aside. Such a firm must notify the FCA of this intention before it exceeds the 20% threshold and must review this decision at least annually. The firm must also advise the FCA if it later considers that the exemption is no longer applicable.

2. Client Money Books and Records

Learning Objective

4.2.1 Know which books and records should be maintained and their function

A regulated firm must maintain a wide range of records to evidence that it has correctly executed its many obligations under the contracts entered into with each of its clients. Each FCA Sourcebook that applies to the firm's business will specify certain records that need to be maintained by the firm – and the firm will also wish to retain any documentation or records that would be necessary to defend itself if a client was to raise a legal claim against the firm.

Where CASS talks about the firm's 'books and records' it does not specifically exclude any of this wider record-keeping; all items form part of the firm's overall books and records. However, CASS 7 does specify two distinct elements that the firm should maintain as part of its overall books and records:

- The client money balance that the firm considers it holds on behalf of each client. The firm should also have records confirming whether this money is held as client money (which reflects whether any exemption has been applied).
- The money that the firm believes should be held in each client bank account and client transaction account used to perform its business.

These are fundamental to evidencing CASS control, in order that the firm can comply with CASS 7.15.12R (a rule applicable to all firms which requires a reconciliation between these two aspects of the firm's internal records – which will be discussed further in section 3 of this chapter).

Both of these internal records may take the form of distinct accounting ledgers, though different firms will use different approaches to maintaining these records, and use different terminology to describe them. We must of course recognise that almost every firm will now use electronic accounting and record-keeping systems rather than manual paper ledgers. As such, there is no standard for the structure of either record. Instead, the firm must ensure that it understands its overall control structures, and ensure that its records contain the information and data necessary for that record to fulfil its function – whether due to a specific CASS control or as part of the firm's wider control environment.

For the purpose of this workbook, it is useful to distinguish these specific aspects from the wider 'records' maintained by the firm. We will, therefore, adopt the following terms (though, as noted above, these are not CASS terms):

- **client ledger** – the specific part(s) of the firm's internal records that confirms the money the firm believes it holds on behalf of each client
- **bank ledger** – the specific part(s) of the firm's internal records that confirms the money the firm believes should be held in each CBA/CTA.

The primary function of the client ledger is to record money received and money paid away in respect of each client. It enables the firm to know the amount of uninvested cash still held for the client, and so is linked to the discharge of fiduciary duty. For example, a cheque might have been issued to a client, but until that cheque has been cleared through the banking system and the money has left the firm's bank account the firm must continue to recognise that the money is client money.

Importantly, the client ledger itself does not need to recognise where this money is being held. Suppose that a firm is using a diversification approach to the client money it holds, and so has client bank accounts open at multiple banks. The client ledger does not need to trace money movements between those CBAs, as such cash movements do not affect the total amount of money that the firm is holding for its client. However, if a firm has a functionally rich ledger recording system it would not be wrong for the firm to include additional information within the client ledger.

The primary function of the bank ledger is to record the money that the firm believes should be held in each CBA and CTA operated. Remember that most firms handling client money will use a number of different client money accounts – passing money between them in line with their own operational structures. It is not sufficient under CASS 7 for the firm to simply track individual client balances and periodically sum the total to check against a bank account statement, even if the firm was only operating using a single CBA.

Where the client ledger must record entries that affect the balance held for each client (for example, transactions undertaken, or cash received or paid out to the client) this bank ledger must record all transactions and movements passing through that CBA or CTA, so must be separately maintained for each account. Note that as the firm will maintain such a ledger in respect of any CBA and CTA held, it is possible that some accounts will not actually reside at a 'bank'. Any circumstances where the difference between a CBA and a CTA becomes important to CASS controls will be highlighted as this chapter progresses.

By maintaining these two 'ledgers' (in whatever manner, and by whatever name) the firm should be able to satisfy two other requirements of CASS. The firm should be able to determine from its internal records (as a whole) the amount of client money it should be holding for each of its clients. In addition, the firm should also be able to determine from its internal records the total value that ought to be held as client money. While CASS allows the firm to use any aspects of its internal records to achieve these goals, the 'client ledger' and 'bank ledger' aspects of those overall internal records should enable the results to be promptly determined.

3. CASS 7 Reconciliations

Learning Objective

4.3.1   Understand the purpose of the internal and external client money reconciliations

4.3.2   Know how often the client money reconciliations must be performed

As noted in section 2, different firms will maintain their internal records in different ways – but for ease of discussion this chapter will continue to use the terms 'client ledger' and 'bank ledger' to describe the particular parts of the firm's records discussed in section 2. Regardless of how any firm chooses to structure (and name) these ledgers, the firm needs to recognise how its records are structured in order to satisfy the reconciliation requirements of CASS.

These two 'ledgers' are central to the firm demonstrating that its organisational arrangements are adequate to minimise the risk of client money being lost. However, it is also important that the firm has controls to ensure that both these ledgers are updated promptly and accurately. For this reason, CASS 7 specifies two reconciliations that must be performed, to ensure that any errors arising within or between these ledgers will be promptly identified and the relevant action taken.

3.1   Internal Client Money Reconciliation

The internal client money reconciliation ensures that the firm's client ledger and bank ledger are aligned with each other, and that any differences are identified, understood, and promptly resolved.

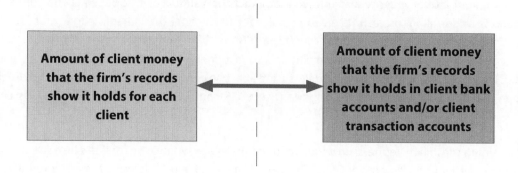

As the two 'ledgers' serve distinct purposes, it is common for different processes within the firm and its systems to affect the balances in each of these records. Where such accounting entries are manual there is a risk that data might be input incorrectly or that certain manual steps within a transaction process could be missed in error. Similarly, system or timing issues could cause the two records to reflect different positions.

CASS requires that the internal client money reconciliation must therefore be performed each day, and should identify cases where incorrect postings are applied to either of these ledgers, as a difference would arise between the total represented by each ledger. (Note: the internal client money reconciliation is not expected to identify all types of error. For example, this reconciliation would not identify any errors where both internal ledgers have been updated incorrectly. Effective CASS control requires multiple different mechanisms to operate correctly.)

The internal client money reconciliation is actually far more technical and complex than this simple headline statement, and we will consider this in detail in the next section of this chapter. However, all firms subject to CASS 7 are required by CASS 7.15.12R to perform a reconciliation between these two records, regardless of the specific method adopted:

> 'An internal client money reconciliation requires a firm to carry out a reconciliation of its internal records and accounts of the amount of client money that the firm holds for each client with its internal records and accounts of the client money that the firm should hold in its client bank accounts or has placed in client transaction accounts.'

It is important that when performing an internal client money reconciliation the firm only uses its internal records. As the regulation quoted above shows, the purpose is to ensure reconciliation between these distinct totals as at close of business on the previous day. This requires the firm to ensure that it has processed all relevant postings for that day, in order that the close of business position will be a reliable representation of all cash movements arising on each ledger.

Note that some types of cash movement cannot be triggered autonomously by the firm. For example, if bank interest is to be received on a given bank account balance, the firm will generally need to wait until such an item has been seen on the external bank account before the corresponding internal ledger entries can be recorded. Identification of such external triggers is therefore necessary to the firm maintaining an accurate record, though the firm should not seek to identify such items as part of its internal client money reconciliation process. Rather, there should be a separate operational process to identify such items and ensure they are correctly and promptly recorded in the firm's records (noting the obligations for allocation of receipts).

3.2   External Client Money Reconciliation

Learning Objective

4.3.3   Be able to apply the external reconciliation requirements

Ensuring that the firm's client ledger aligns with its bank ledger is only part of the story. We have just considered that some items will first be identified when a transaction is processed on the bank account statement. If the firm fails to identify such activity, and so fails to update both its client ledger and bank ledger, those records will remain aligned even though the additional transaction has been missed. The internal client money reconciliation would not identify the problem.

Also, depending upon how the firm's systems process market transactions, it could be possible for a market transaction executed by the firm to be miskeyed in the firm's internal records – such that the bank ledger reflects the wrong settlement figure for the aggregated trade, and the system allocates that same wrong figure between the relevant clients. Again, the internal records will reconcile, though the actual money moving in the bank accounts will disagree.

That is the purpose behind the external client money reconciliation:

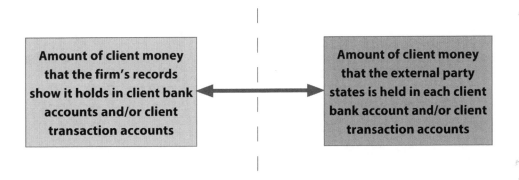

The external client money reconciliation identifies the amount of client money that the firm's internal records state should be segregated as client money and compares it against the amount of client money that the relevant external bank account statements state is segregated as client money.

While the internal client money reconciliation must be performed each day, the CASS rules require the firm to determine the most appropriate frequency for performing an external client money reconciliation. The firm should complete this reconciliation '…*as regularly as is necessary…*' to ensure proper controls, with a maximum period of one month between reconciliations. Guidance within CASS 7 adds that most firms performing daily transactions should perform the external client money reconciliation each business day.

Practitioners should be aware of a complexity they face as they transition from study to the operation of CASS controls. Individuals must recognise that certain aspects of CASS rules do require a firm to make a clear interpretation as to how it will proceed. In most cases, this reflects flexibility permitted by the rules, and the range of activity that different firms might undertake, though in some cases the wording is harder to understand. CASS 7.15.27R is an example of the latter. However, the key aspects recorded in this rule are:

- both CBAs and CTAs are relevant
- each currency and each bank account should be reviewed
- the reconciliation involves the firm's record of that currency/account and the most recent statement/confirmation received from the bank (for a CBA) or third party (for a CTA), and
- any discrepancies identified should be resolved promptly.

The external client money reconciliation should therefore complement the internal client money reconciliation, as any error made in the firm's ledgers (or indeed any error made in the bank's records) should be identifiable in either one or both of these reconciliation controls. However, it is important to note that these ledger controls are not expected to identify any situations where the firm has actually executed a deal incorrectly in the market. Suppose a client instructed the firm to purchase shares to a value of £10,000 – but the firm incorrectly executes a deal to the value of £1,000. All downstream ledger processing should reflect the transaction as executed (the value of £1,000), which will agree with the value settled in the CBA/CTA. As such, neither the internal nor external reconciliations will identify that the original transaction execution was incorrect. It is therefore important to note that CASS controls are not intended to identify all potential problems; rather, the CASS rules should ensure that the firm correctly segregates money according to the actual activity it has undertaken, to detect and resolve any errors made when recording such executions in the firm's ledgers, and to identify any errors made by any third party holding client money on account for the firm.

4. The Standard Methods of Client Money Reconciliation

Learning Objective

4.4.1 Understand the difference between the standard methods and non-standard methods of internal client money reconciliation

4.4.2 Be able to apply the standard methods of internal client money reconciliation

4.4.3 Understand how to deal with reconciliation discrepancies

We have already noted that the CASS rules do not define a single operational response from all regulated firms, but instead represent a set of rules that a firm must understand when making decisions about how client money will be processed and controlled while in the company's care. In the same way, CASS 7.15 sets out the essential obligations of the CASS rules in respect of client money reconciliations. Each firm holding client money must ensure that its controls satisfy these obligations. However, because of the potential diversity of operational approaches, the potential complexity of the underlying accounting processes, and the importance of enabling a successful CASS audit each year, section 7.16 of CASS sets out particular approaches that a firm can adopt to satisfy its CASS 7.15 obligations.

Even within these approaches, the firm can make choices as to how certain calculations are performed. Consequently, the approaches set out in CASS 7.16 are referred to as 'the **standard methods** of client money reconciliation'. If the firm devises some other way of achieving the requirements of CASS 7.15 that does not apply the methodology in CASS 7.16, the firm is said to be using 'a non-standard method of internal client money reconciliation'.

The following diagram illustrates the key structural choices that a firm has made to this point:

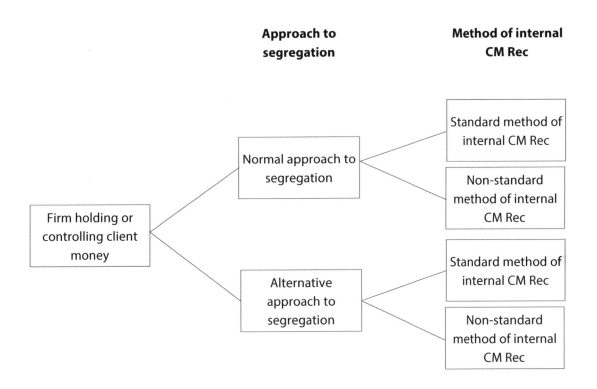

In this section, we will unpack the practical implications of this choice between a standard method of internal client money reconciliation and a non-standard method.

There are some aspects of the internal client money reconciliation that apply in both cases:

- It must be performed each business day.
- It is performed using the firm's internal records as at close of business on the prior business day.
- It must include a calculation of the client money **resource** and client money **requirement** – two specific terms defined in the FCA Glossary and explained in detail in CASS. In simple terms, the client money resource is the amount that the firm's internal ledgers state should be segregated as client money within its CBAs (ie, it is derived from the firm's bank ledgers). The client money requirement is the amount that the firm's internal ledgers state the firm ought to have segregated as client money because of client activity and certain other sums.
- Any discrepancy between the client money resource and client money requirement needs to be investigated once discovered, and action taken that same day to resolve it.

The below table sets out how discrepancies must be resolved:

Result of Internal CM Rec	Known as	Consequence
Resource is greater than requirement	An 'excess'	The firm must post the entries needed to resolve the excess sum within its ledgers. This may simply require the firm to post a ledger item missed in error on the previous day (for example, reducing the bank ledger, or increasing the sum allocated to a particular client). In some cases, the firm's investigations may also recognise a need to remove money from the actual CBA.
Requirement is greater than resource	A 'shortfall'	The firm must post the entries needed to resolve the shortfall position – which may for example have been caused by the firm not recording a discharge of fiduciary duty in its client ledger (such that the requirement calculation is too high) or by failing to record a bank receipt where the corresponding client-level record was created on the previous day. Again, in some cases, the firm's investigations will show that it must pay actual money into a CBA as part of resolving this discrepancy.
Resource equals requirement	Balanced	There is no internal reconciliation discrepancy (as in this context CASS uses the word 'discrepancy' to identify an imbalance between the resource and requirement figures calculated). However, it is possible that performing the internal client money reconciliation could still identify some processing error to be rectified – even if that processing error does not result in a 'discrepancy' as per CASS 7.

Note that the FCA's Glossary definitions for resource and requirement emphasise that they are total/ aggregated figures for the firm. Therefore, each day, the firm should determine its final total resource and requirement figures, although separate component figures will be used as part of the calculation. Where a shortfall is identified, the rules allow it to be addressed by paying corporate money into any one of the firm's CBAs.

The term 'standard method' effectively relates to the calculations performed by the firm to determine the client money requirement and client money resource from its internal ledgers. We will see that there are two standard methods of calculating the client money requirement and one standard method of calculating the client money resource. If the firm decides to calculate these values using any other method, then the firm is said to be using a 'non-standard method' – which requires prior approval from its auditor and notification to the FCA.

4.1   Client Money Resource

Under the standard method, the client money resource is effectively the aggregate balance the firm has recorded that it ought to hold in its CBAs. This initially sounds simple, but we must remember two things:

- As this is part of the internal client money reconciliation, this calculation must be performed using the firm's internal bank records, and not using bank statements.
- In deciding when to effect postings to its bank ledger, the firm needs to consider whether the money is actually expected to be on the account yet.

For instance, if the firm's business model includes receiving cheques or pure cash from its clients, then such money will only be within a CBA once the firm has banked the money. Therefore, if the firm has not yet banked a cheque, it should not include the value of that cheque in its client money resource.

It should be noted that CASS does not make any comment requiring the firm to wait until it believes the cheque has been cleared before including it in the client money resource; once banked the money should be included.

It is necessary to make an observation about CTAs, because the FCA's wording appears inconsistent. We have already noted that CASS 7.15.12R requires the internal reconciliation to include client money held in both CBAs and CTAs, yet the glossary definition of client money resource states that the term relates only to money held in CBAs. CASS 7.16.8R describes the way to determine the client money resource under the 'standard method', and again states that only the CBAs should be included. We will note in section 4.2 how the calculation of client money requirement is affected by CTAs; for the moment it is sufficient to highlight the interpretative tension affecting a firm that uses CTAs in its business model.

Clarity over the operational interactions between the CTAs and the firm's CBAs and corporate accounts is likely to be key to a firm making this decision, and the firm must be ready to explain its decision to its auditor.

4.2   Client Money Requirement

CASS states that, under the standard method, the client money requirement should be the total amount of client money a firm is required to have segregated in CBAs in accordance with the client money rules. This wording is subtle, as it means that the client money requirement is not simply the sum of money that the firm has allocated to each client. The phrase 'segregated...in accordance with the client money rules' means that other sums of money – including money not allocated to individual clients – must also be included in the client money requirement if the firm's application of CASS rules means that the firm should have segregated that sum.

As with the client money resource calculation, the client money requirement is an aggregate figure across the firm's business, though the standard method of internal client money reconciliation offers two methods by which a firm might determine its client money requirement.

The first of these methods, known as the **individual client balance (ICB) method** is available to all types of firm other than a loan-based crowdfunding firm. In simple terms, the individual client balance method requires the firm to determine the amount of client money it should be holding for each separate client (across all products and accounts that the firm operates in respect of that client), and then perform a calculation based on those figures. Importantly, as we will see in detail shortly, when applying the ICB method the firm must ignore any client balances that are negative. To complete the requirement calculation, the firm must then reflect any other sums that it believes ought to be segregated as client money; as such sums are not allocated to individual clients those amounts have not yet been included within the aggregate figure being determined.

The second method is known as the **net negative add-back (NNAB) method**, and it is only available to the loan-based crowdfunding firms (ie, those prohibited from using the individual client balance method) or CASS 7 asset management firms (a specific FCA-defined term, representing firms that receive income primarily from activities such as managing investments, providing platform services, safeguarding and administering investments, or acting as the authorised fund manager (AFM) of collective investment schemes).

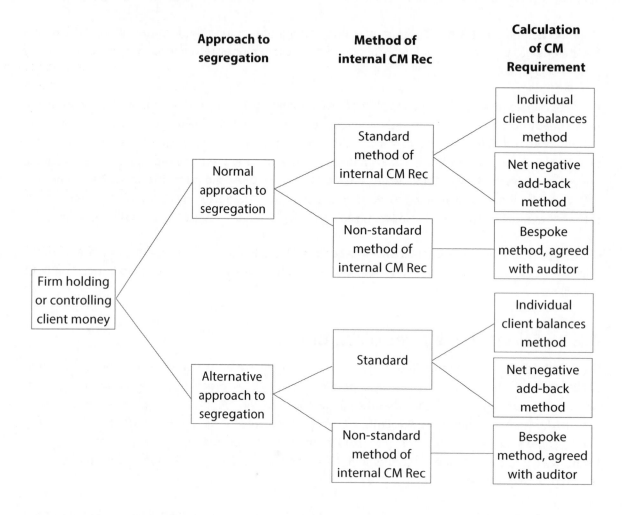

In simple terms, the NNAB calculation requires the firm to start with the total amount of money the firm believes it is holding in its CBAs, and add onto that total amount a sum equivalent to the value of any net overdrawn cash position currently maintained for any individual client, ie, the value of the overdrawn balance is 'added back' onto the total figure (as it has effectively been deducted within the calculation of the account balance). The ICB method requires the firm to add into its requirement calculation various items that are not allocated to an individual client (such as unallocated monies, or sums held as prudent segregation). Unless such items are specifically added, the requirement figure would be too small. The NNAB method differs as it starts with the firm's record of the CBA balance, so should include such items even though they are not allocated to an individual client. As such, a firm using the NNAB method need only ensure that such items have been included in the internal records used to begin the calculation, rather than adding in such items later in the calculation.

We will now explore both methods in greater detail. As noted above, certain types of firm will only be permitted to apply one of these methods, while other types of firm will be able to choose from either method. Having determined which method it will use, the firm will ensure that data reporting and system extracts will provide the data necessary to accurately perform the relevant calculation method.

4.2.1   Individual Client Balance (ICB) Method

When using this method, the first step to calculating the client money requirement is to determine the amount of client money that the firm considers it should have segregated for each client. The calculation of individual client balances can either be performed:

a.   separately for each of the firm's business lines or products, or
b.   across all products and services that the firm operates.

However, the final calculation of the client money requirement must then determine the single total figure for the firm.

Having calculated the underlying ICB figures, all the positive balances are added together. Negative balances are ignored because firms are not permitted to extend a credit line using client money, so including them would reduce the total value of the requirement figure, which would result in less client money remaining segregated.

Suppose that the firm offers a general investment account (GIA), a stocks and shares individual savings accounts (ISAs), and a non-insurance pension product, and its client ledger shows the following amounts of uninvested cash:

Investor	GIA	ISA	Pension
A	250	50	50
B	−50	0	200
C	−125	25	0
D	200	125	75
E	250	150	100
F	−325	50	25
G	100	75	125
H	−100	50	100
I	400	50	0
J	100	0	0

To use the ICB method, the firm must first determine the total amount held for each client.

Investor	GIA	ISA	Pension	Total
A	250	50	50	350
B	−50	0	200	150
C	−125	25	0	−100
D	200	125	75	400
E	250	150	100	500
F	−325	50	25	−250
G	100	75	125	300
H	−100	50	100	50
I	400	50	0	450
J	100	0	0	100
			Total	**£1,950**

Here we see the total uninvested cash balance held for each person, which totals £1,950.

However, £1,950 is not the value the firm needs, because two of the clients have a net negative balance across their products. Under the ICB method, clients having a negative overall balance (in respect of the product lines being considered at the time) are excluded. Our current example is determining client balances across all products and services, and so the firm's calculation will instead look like this.

Investor	GIA	ISA	Pension	Total	Requirement
A	250	50	50	350	350
B	−50	0	200	150	150
C	−125	25	0	−100	0
D	200	125	75	400	400
E	250	150	100	500	500
F	−325	50	25	−250	0
G	100	75	125	300	300
H	−100	50	100	50	50
I	400	50	0	450	450
J	100	0	0	100	100
				Total	**£2,300**

By taking only the positive balances, the amount of money that must be segregated for clients is increased – which makes sense because the intention is to ensure that all clients would receive back from the segregated account any money due to them. Even though the firm has potentially only permitted a client to become overdrawn because some asset position is held instead, CASS requires the firm to ensure that the total amount of money segregated will cover the total sum of client money due to its customers.

Note that investor H's balance remains in the calculation – despite having an overdrawn balance associated with the general investment account – because here we are illustrating the approach in which all products and services are being included together. In that context, it is the client's net balance across all products and services that determines whether their balance is included, regardless of any underlying negative balances in an individual product. If the firm considers its products and services in a number of smaller packets, it is the client's net balance in respect of each set of products that determines whether their balance would be included in respect of that set of products.

Given the range of postings that may affect a client's balance, CASS sets out the following calculation that firms should perform when calculating the client balance of each individual:

Free money (sums held for a client free of sale or purchase (eg, see (3)(a)) and	A
sale proceeds due to the client:	
a. for principal deals when the client has delivered the designated investments, and	B
b. for agency deals, when:	
1. the sale proceeds have been received by the firm and the client has delivered the designated investments, or	C1
2. the firm holds the designated investments for the client, and	C2
the cost of purchases:	
c. for principal deals, paid for by the client when the firm has not delivered the designated investments to the client, and	D
d. for agency deals, paid for by the client when:	
1. the firm has not remitted the money to, or to the order of, the counterparty, or	E1
2. the designated investments have been received by the firm but have not been delivered to the client	E2
Less	
money owed by the client for unpaid purchases by, or for, the client if delivery of those designated investments has been made to the client, and	F
proceeds remitted to the client for sales transactions by, or for, the client if the client has not delivered the designated investments.	G
Individual client balance 'X' = (A+B+C1+C2+D+E1+E2)–F–G	X

Note that the context in which asset transactions are undertaken becomes relevant to how such money is considered. This largely arises because the market settlement is likely to take a different approach – including the money movements required to enable settlement. Again, firms must understand their own systems, processes, and ledger postings in order to be confident that they are complying with CASS.

4.2.2   Net Negative Add-Back (NNAB) Method

The NNAB method determines the client money requirement in a different way. Some types of business do not intend to hold uninvested cash for their customers, and so the individual client balances would usually be zero for all clients. Loan-based crowdfunding firms are required to use the NNAB method, while CASS 7 asset management firms are able to choose this method instead of the ICB method if they so wish (a decision that will usually be determined by the operations of their internal cash systems – another example of CASS giving flexibility as to how a firm will achieve compliance with the rules).

On the basis that any cash balance is likely to be an exception case, NNAB does not add up the balances held for each client. Rather, it starts from the figure that the firm believes is segregated as client money, ie, it starts with the bank ledger for each CBA used by the firm. The calculation of client money requirement under the NNAB method is undertaken bank account by bank account.

Suppose that a given firm produces an extract from its client records, confirming that the following clients have overdrawn positions in certain products:

Investor	GIA	ISA	Pension
B	−50	0	200
C	−125	25	0
F	−325	50	25
H	−100	50	100

In some cases, a firm might use a different CBA for each product, or might for operational reasons use one CBA to collect client money while using a different CBA for payments of client money (and perhaps a third CBA to hold monies currently under investigation and resolution). Where a firm uses multiple CBAs under the NNAB method, it would need to determine the negative balances against each (though at the end of the process, the firm will still need to aggregate its client money requirement figure in line with the definition). To keep this example simple however, let us assume that this particular firm runs its business using a single CBA.

The NNAB method requires the firm to determine which clients have a net negative balance in respect of that CBA. Let us assume that the firm's bank ledger shows that this particular CBA has a balance of £1,950:

Total CM per bank ledger   £1,950

The following investors have negative balances on products:

Investor	GIA	ISA	Pension	Total
B	−50	0	200	150
C	−125	25	0	−100
F	−325	50	25	−250
H	−100	50	100	50

The NNAB method requires the firm to 'add back' onto the corresponding bank ledger balance the value of any net negative client balances associated with that CBA. In this case, two clients have a net negative balance, and so those amounts must be added back onto the ledger balance to ensure that all underlying positive client balances will be sufficiently segregated.

Total CM per bank ledger   £1,950

The following investors have negative balances on products:

Investor	GIA	ISA	Pension	Total	NNAB
B	−50	0	200	150	0
C	−125	25	0	−100	100
F	−325	50	25	−250	250
H	−100	50	100	50	0

                                          Total   £350

              Figure needed for requirement calculation   £2,300

You may have noticed that both the examples above were based upon the same underlying client data – so, for this simple scenario of a single CBA, both calculations should arrive at the same conclusion.

Note also that if a firm using the NNAB method does operate multiple CBAs, the above calculation would need to be repeated for each of those CBAs (as required by CASS 7.16.17R). Having performed the NNAB calculation on each CBA, CASS 7.16.17R also confirms that the firm must add together those figures in order to determine the actual 'requirement' for the firm. The firm will still have a single 'resource' and a single 'requirement' figure on each day.

4.2.3   Additional Steps to Calculate the CM Requirement – Both Methods

In a simple scenario, both these methods would yield the same result. The two examples above are based on the same underlying client data, and in the absence of any other considerations both methods would provide the same result. However, there are other considerations that need to be included within the firm's daily calculation of its requirement figure – and these will depend significantly upon the specific accounting and ledger posting approach taken by a firm. Note also that in satisfying the following points, each firm will only need to take the steps necessary in respect of the method it has selected (either NNAB or ICB).

The CASS rules at first appear vague in respect of these items – but as we will see this is simply a reflection of the fact that a firm using ICB must act in one way while a firm using NNAB may need to act in another way.

The following table offers some comments on the additional factors that a firm must consider. While some of these observations may at first appear obvious, the firm must understand its underlying ledger processing to ensure that the calculation of its requirement figure achieves the correct outcomes.

Factor	Impact within ICB method	Impact within NNAB method
Segregated money not associated to individual clients: • unidentified/unallocated monies • prudent segregation • sums to cover unresolved client asset shortfall, where not attributed to individual clients.	As such money is not allocated to a client, the firm must add such money to its requirement calculation.	As such money should already be contained in the firm's bank ledger, the firm must ensure the money remains in the requirement calculation, which may require an adjustment to be made if it is not already posted.
Cash/cheques received, but not yet banked.	CASS recognises that some firms might allocate such sums to client accounts upon receipt, while others may allocate the money to the client's account only once deposited at the bank. Either is acceptable but the firm must consider its ledgers. Such money is not banked, so will not be included in the resource calculation. If such sums are initially included in the requirement calculation (ie, within the ICB or NNAB calculation), the firm is required to deduct such sums before finalising its client money requirement for that day. Firms should therefore consider the complexity of this step (and the need to maintain a record of such unbanked items) when determining the timing of their ledger postings.	
Cheques/payable orders issued but not yet paid by the bank.	Again, firms may operate their ledger postings in different ways. However, such sums must remain part of the client money requirement until the associated fiduciary duty has been discharged.	
Client money held in respect of non-margined transactions.	The firm must take into account all client money it ought to hold in connection with non-margined transactions. Guidance in CASS 7.16.27G effectively means that monies held in a CTA are excluded from each component of the requirement calculation.	CASS requires that such money must remain included in the requirement calculation regardless of the party holding the money. While this at first may seem simple, it can be a complicated consideration given the wide range of approaches that a firm might take to the execution and settlement of transactions.

4.2.4 Inclusion of Margined Transactions within the Client Money Requirement

Learning Objective

4.4.4 Know what the margined transaction requirement is

So far, we have looked at simple asset transactions, where a few days after trade date the asset is exchanged for money. However, there are other types of transaction (such as those involving financial futures) that create potential future liabilities between the parties to the contract. To reduce the risk of default on such transactions the parties agree to exchange some money during the time until the transaction is completed. Such payments are known as 'margin' payments (they cover the gap between trade date and settlement date). We will discuss such margined transactions later in the workbook (chapter 5, section 4).

As regards the client money requirement, in the context of this workbook it is sufficient to note that CASS requires a firm to make a calculation relating to client money held in respect of such transactions.

The margined transaction requirement represents the amount of money that the firm would need to pay out to the client, minus amounts already set aside by the firm in client transaction accounts or other collateral, if the client's positions were all closed out at the end of the previous business day (calculated at that day's closing prices). Where a firm is undertaking margined transactions for its clients, it must calculate this 'margined transaction requirement' and include the amount in the client money requirement before the firm finalises its figure for a given day. Firms undertaking margined transactions must perform the ICB method of client money requirement calculation.

End of Chapter Questions

Think of an answer for each question and refer to the appropriate section for confirmation

1. What four elements does CASS recommend be part of a firm's due diligence on the banks or third parties holding its client money?
    Answer reference: Section 1

2. What two specific aspects of the firm's books and records does CASS 7 require?
    Answer reference: Section 2

3. In simple terms, what is an internal client money reconciliation and how often should it be performed?
    Answer reference: Section 3.1

4. What is an external client money reconciliation, and how often should it be performed?
    Answer reference: Section 3.2

5. Under the standard methods of internal client money reconciliation, what are the client money resource and client money requirement?
    Answer reference: Section 4

6. What is meant by a client money 'excess', and what action must the firm take to resolve an 'excess'?
    Answer reference: Section 4

7. Within the standard methods of internal client money reconciliation, what are the two ways that the firm can calculate its client money requirement?
    Answer reference: Section 4.2

8. What type of firm is not permitted to adopt the individual client balance (ICB) method when calculating its client money requirement?
    Answer reference: 4.2

9. When calculating its client money requirement, how should a firm treat any cash/cheques received from a client but not yet deposited at the bank?
    Answer reference: 4.2.3

10. Where a firm performs margined transactions for its client, how should this affect the calculation of client money requirement?
    Answer reference: 4.2

Chapter Five

Safe Custody Fundamentals (CASS 6)

This syllabus area will provide approximately 5 of the 50 examination questions

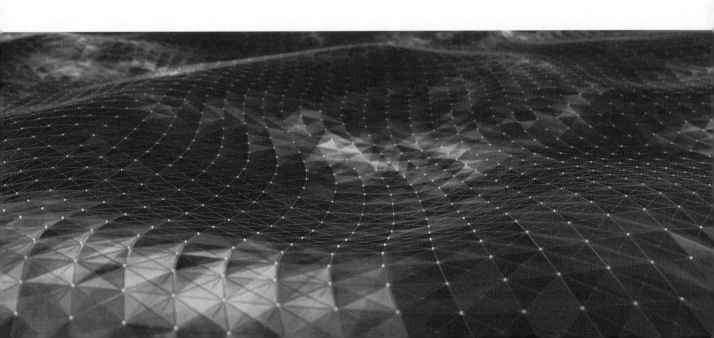

Introduction

We have now looked in detail at the way that client money is protected. A range of mechanisms are at work: segregation of the money upon receipt, records of allocation, the reconciliation controls that ensure that any errors are promptly identified and resolved, and the firm's obligation to resolve any shortfall or excess identified in the daily internal client money reconciliation. All of these ensure that the trust is sound.

We will now explore the parallel considerations and controls that apply to safe custody of client assets held by the firm. Again, we will first consider how the rules function, and then look at the exemptions that are available to certain types of firm.

1. Safe Custody: What It Is

Learning Objective

5.1.1   Understand the requirements for the segregation of safe custody assets

In chapter 1, we established many foundations relating to 'safe custody'; we noted that 'legal title' to transferable securities is recorded in a register maintained by the issuer of the asset, and that firms holding assets on behalf of their clients will commonly use a nominee company to segregate client assets from any assets of the firm. While client safe custody assets are not held within a 'statutory trust' (unlike client money), it remains critical that client safe custody assets are clearly distinct from any custody assets belonging to the firm itself. The use of a nominee company can assist in this segregation, while also being beneficial in the event of the regulated firm becoming insolvent (as the client safe custody assets would be held in the name of the nominee rather than the regulated firm). We will see that there are specific rules that govern the names in which a firm can hold assets within a chain of custody.

We also noted that firms may sometimes retain the services of a specialist custodian in order to hold asset positions on their behalf.

This creates what is known as the 'chain of custody', where multiple parties each maintain records relating to the holdings of their own clients, and travelling along the chain eventually brings us back to the source register of the asset.

Consider, for example, a share traded through a Central Securities Depositary (CSD). While there is an official register for the company shares, the CSD holds a number of those shares and enables trading between firms. Such firms may include custodians, each of which is acting for multiple customers (such as fund managers, pension funds, institutions, and platform providers). Eventually, the chain ends with the actual investors, who each have beneficial ownership of the asset though they will not be the registered owner.

The following diagram illustrates such a chain of custody:

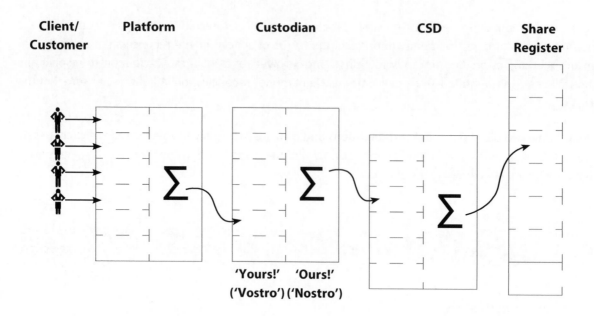

Note that each firm down the chain of custody is operating a set of distinct client accounts, each of which feeds into an aggregated position that is reflected by the next link in the chain. Many firms effectively have distinct nostro and vostro records (see chapter 1, section 3.1 for explanation) with nostro reflecting their overall corporate position and vostro reflecting the holdings of that firm's different clients. If the platform firm illustrated above also holds its own assets with the same custodian, the firm would need to open at least two accounts at the custodian – enabling a clear segregation between its aggregated client safe custody holdings and its aggregated corporate assets. The fact that the custodian's holding at the CSD might itself be an aggregate holding across those multiple vostro accounts does not change the need for the platform to ensure segregation of its holdings at the custodian.

Note also that if the Platform firm in the above illustration were to fail and its records became inaccessible, no other party down the chain would be able to associate any holding with the underlying customer. Where the firm aggregates its position as a single holding at the next entity down the chain of custody, failure at any level will result in problems reuniting a client with the assets being held on their behalf, ie, at each link in the chain, the firm is protecting a safe custody asset on behalf of its client.

In this chapter, we will look at the CASS requirements for such safe custody positions, including the relevant regulatory permissions, the selection and appointment of custodians, and the records and reconciliations that each firm should maintain and perform in order to secure the clarity of entitlement down the length of the custody chain.

At times, the relationships being discussed can get confusing, because each firm down a custody chain is effectively acting as custodian to its clients. For the purposes of this chapter, therefore, we will focus on the situation where Dependable Investments ltd contracts with Strong Custodians ltd, because it wishes to deposit the safe custody assets of its clients with a specialist third-party custodian organisation.

You will recognise that many of the expectations CASS places on a firm in respect of safe custody assets mirror the requirements we have discussed in respect of client money.

2. Holding Client Assets

Learning Objective

5.2.1 Know the obligations created by the permissions: safeguarding and administration of assets (without arranging); arranging safeguarding and administration

5.2.2 Understand the different legal obligations that arise in respect of custody relationships

5.2.3 Understand the implications and risks of intragroup models and third-party appointments

5.2.4 Understand firms' responsibilities in respect of the selection, appointment and review of a third-party custodian

The firm must perform due diligence on any third-party custodian it intends to appoint in respect of client safe custody assets. The firm should exercise due skill, care, and diligence in the selection, appointment and periodic review of the third party and the arrangements to protect client assets.

CASS includes guidance which notes that the firm should consider the following:

- how well the third party has performed its services to the firm
- the overall arrangements to hold safe custody assets
- any standardised accreditations/certifications that the third party holds
- the capital and/or financial resources of the third party
- whether the third party is creditworthy
- the breadth of the third party's activities (potentially including any affiliated companies), and
- whether the third party holds the relevant regulatory permissions.

As always, compliance requires a firm to be able to demonstrate the actions it took, and so the firm should retain formal records of these initial and periodic assessments, retaining such records for five years after the firm ceases to use the third party concerned.

2.1 Regulated Activities relating to Safe Custody

Chapter 2 introduced the Financial Conduct Authority (FCA) permissions, and noted that there are two separate activities relating to safe custody assets:

- arranging safeguarding and administration of assets
- safeguarding and administering of assets (without arranging).

In simple terms, the FCA considers that there are two distinct types of work that a custodian performs. 'Safeguarding' relates to protecting the asset from harm or damage. Where an asset is in physical form (such as a bearer share), the custodian provides a facility to keep that document safe. For example, it would use fireproof safes and other security measures to protect the integrity of the document. 'Administration' of the asset relates to the consequential aspects that arise from investments – such as collecting dividends and other income events, or handling corporate actions that may arise. Administration of assets is essentially ensuring that the client receives all applicable entitlements, despite the fact that the asset will usually have been registered within the custodian's nominee name rather than the client's own name.

Having established 'safeguarding' and 'administration', we must next understand what is meant by 'arranging' or 'without arranging'. The best way to approach this is by looking at two different business models that a firm might adopt.

Suppose that Dependable Investments ltd ('Dependable') sets up a product that allows the clients to buy and sell a range of assets, with product terms and conditions stating how the assets will be held.

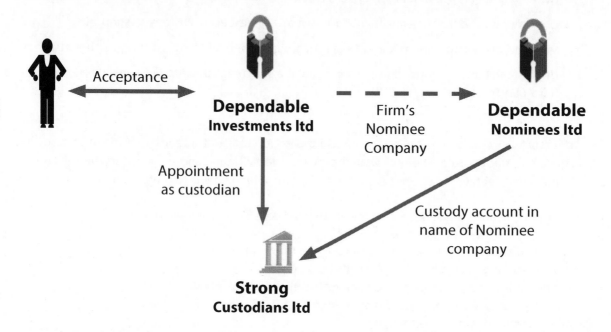

We can see that Dependable is taking ownership of assets on behalf of its customer; holding those assets in its own Nominee company name. While Dependable has appointed a third-party custodian, opening an account at the custodian in the name of Dependable Nominees ltd, the fact remains that Dependable is itself responsible to its clients for the safeguarding and administration of the assets held on their behalf. In such a model, Dependable would be performing the activity of safeguarding and administration of assets (without arranging), even though the use of a third-party custodian means that the third party is safeguarding and administering the assets on behalf of Dependable and the other clients of that third-party custodian. The contract between Dependable and its clients makes it clear that Dependable is responsible for the assets.

However, it is also possible to adopt an alternative custody structure, which would operate as follows. Suppose that Dependable Investments ltd creates a product that allows the clients to buy and sell a range of assets, again governed by a set of terms and conditions. However, in this case, those terms and conditions state that Dependable will open a custody account at Strong Custodians ltd ('Strong') for each investor that applies. Importantly, each of those accounts would be opened in the name of the investor concerned, and not in the name of either Dependable Investments ltd or its nominee company (as the nominee company is only required if the firm is holding assets for its clients). Dependable will use the consent provided by the client in the complete application form to introduce or arrange for that client to directly become a customer of Strong Custodians ltd. Trade instructions would be subject to the Dependable terms and conditions, while the custody arrangements would be governed by separate Strong terms and conditions relating to what is a separate contract.

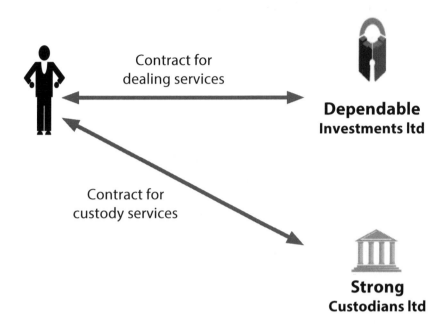

Dependable, therefore, has no ongoing obligations for the safeguarding and administration of the assets traded; it simply arranges for the custody service to be put in place (which might include paying any service charges arising).

As we continue to explore the types of CASS controls that need to be put in place to protect client safe custody assets – controls such as segregation and reconciliation – it is worth noting that a firm that only arranges safeguarding and administration of assets would naturally have no obligations in respect of segregation and reconciliation, as the firm holds no assets to segregate or reconcile.

In some cases, the two companies combining their efforts to service the client may be part of the same corporate group, ie, sister companies within one large financial institution. However, as we saw from the outset, client asset rules exist to manage the risk of loss that materialises following the failure of a specific legal entity. Therefore, under either of the models illustrated above, each firm must consider its own regulatory and servicing obligations regardless of the potential that individual services are being provided by a different legal entity from within the same corporate group.

The term 'intragroup' is sometimes used to indicate a servicing structure in which two legal entities from the same financial institution each perform certain duties associated with their respective regulatory authorisations. Where the firm has appointed a third party to act as its custodian, it usually follows that the firm will also have obligations to its clients (as the custodian account will normally be in the name of the firm or its nominee company). From a CASS perspective, each firm operating in an intragroup model must exercise the same level of care and due diligence as it would when working alongside any independent provider.

Note also that this section relates to the distinction between the two FCA permissions relating to custody services, and whether the firm has any contractual obligations for the assets. This distinction is separate from the question of whether a firm has 'outsourced' or 'delegated' the performance of certain operational tasks to a different entity. We will discuss the consequences of outsourcing in chapter 7 of this workbook.

2.2 International Considerations

Learning Objective

5.2.5 Understand the rules concerning depositing assets outside of the UK

The requirements for protecting client safe custody assets apply regardless of the jurisdiction in which that asset might be held. However, the CASS rules recognise that as market practices and domestic law may differ in certain jurisdictions it is necessary to provide some additional flexibility to firms in some situations.

One example is the **registration** and recording of legal title. CASS 6 notes that in some jurisdictions it might not be possible to hold certain assets in the name of the client or a suitable nominee company. Where such approaches are not possible (not simply that the firm would prefer to use a different approach), CASS will permit the firm to apply a different registration method.

The firm might use the services of a third party to hold the assets (without utilising a nominee company) – if the firm is prevented from using either of the above approaches, and is not a trustee firm. The firm must have assessed whether proceeding in the proposed way remains in the client's best interests, and the firm must notify the client in writing that proceeding will mean that the assets will not be protected in the usual manner.

Finally – and only if none of the approaches already noted are legally achievable – CASS will allow the firm to hold the assets in its own name. This would require prior consent from a retail client, though if servicing a professional client it is sufficient for the firm to notify that client of the circumstances which will apply.

2.3 Third-Party Custody Agreements

Learning Objective

5.2.6 Understand the requirements for third-party custody agreements

CASS requires that the firm enter into a written agreement with any third party with whom it either arranges the custody of client safe custody assets or who holds such assets on the firm's behalf. The agreement must be binding in legal terms and clearly set out the custody service being performed during the period while the assets are held.

Guidance in CASS highlights certain types of clauses that the firm should consider when entering into such an agreement. These include operational factors (such as the procedures and authorities governing instructions between the parties), service limitations (such as any restrictions on the ability to withdraw assets), and matters relating to how the firm's holdings will be recorded within the custodian's own records (and how the custodian will register the assets in the next link of the custody chain).

Liability is another important aspect, given that the custodian is the external interface for settling transactions and receiving income due on holdings. The agreement should specify how income will be claimed and received (whether dividends, interest, or other types of payment), as well as establishing the third party's liability in the event of an asset being lost due to fraud, wilful default or negligence.

The CASS rules also emphasise that the custody agreement should not grant a lien, set-off right, or security interest over client safe custody assets unless such a right relates specifically to debts incurred by the third party in the performance of its work for that client. Effectively this is a contractual equivalent to the trust acknowledgement letter discussed earlier in the context of client bank accounts. The custodian must accept and acknowledge in the contract that it cannot simply take over the assets it holds for the firm in respect of the firm's clients.

3. Exemptions

Learning Objective

5.3.1 Understand the use of exemptions available within the custody rules

Once a firm has decided upon its business model and the authorisations necessary to put that model into effect, the firm will be able to determine whether CASS 6 (the custody rules) as a whole is applicable to that business model. We have seen that firms which are only arranging for another entity to perform safeguarding and administration of assets will have fewer obligations under the rules as the firm itself does not 'hold' any assets for its clients.

However, even once a firm has concluded that CASS 6 is relevant to its business, there are some specific exemptions that can be applied to certain scenarios and transactions.

3.1 Business in the Name of the Firm

We have seen that the firm might not be 'safeguarding and administering investments', in which case it would not be responsible for any assets subject to CASS 6.

CASS 6 specifically notes that some types of transaction the firm might perform on behalf of its clients might require the firm to carry on business in its own name. The example given in CASS 6 is if the firm borrows safe custody assets from a client as principal under a stock-lending agreement.

We will discuss stock lending in chapter 7 of the workbook, along with other types of activity involving collateral.

3.2 Temporary Handling

There are occasions when a firm might need to receive some asset from its client in order to undertake the proposed service. For example, if a firm's business model does not include any services relating to the holding of physical assets (such that the firm would not need to maintain any documentation or policy in respect of a physical asset reconciliation).

Suppose that one of the firm's clients then sends a physical share certificate to the firm, explaining that they found the investment and want the firm to add the shares into the investment portfolio being managed/administered by the firm. While the firm had not intended to service physical assets, they are now in possession of one. CASS 6 grants an exemption in such cases, applicable providing the firm is not going to hold the asset for a prolonged period. If the asset will only be held by the firm for a short time – long enough simply to fulfil the client's instructions – then this 'temporary handling' exemption can be used, removing the need to build full-strength capabilities to hold and administer physical assets.

A firm using the 'temporary handling' exemption is not able to ignore the risks presented by it receiving this asset – the firm is still subject to Principle 10 – but the operational requirements are simplified. The firm must take four key actions:

- Keep the asset secure while it is in the firm's possession.
- Record that the asset belongs to the specific client.
- Act on the client's instructions as soon as practicable.
- Make and retain a record of the asset that has been handled, together with details of the client and the actions taken.

This last point might at first seem to merely duplicate the items above. However, the key point here is the need for the firm to maintain a formal record of the events. Each year, the firm's CASS audit will review the controls in place, and so any firm that has been using the temporary handling exemption will need to demonstrate to its auditor that the correct actions were taken.

3.3   Managers of AIFs and UCITS

Alternative investment funds (AIFs) and undertakings for collective investment in transferable securities (UCITS) are two terms used to define types of collective investment schemes (CISs). While the terms were originally used in EU Directives, they remain part of the UK rules.

There is an exemption in CASS 6 addressed to the regulated firms that manage such CISs. It should be noted that this exemption is only expressed as guidance within CASS 6 – indicating that the guidance paragraph is merely confirming something that ought to be identifiable from an individual rule. Again, the basis of the exemption is to understand the firm's activity and the role it is performing. The manager of a CIS is always balancing obligations in two different contexts:

- what is happening inside the fund's investment portfolio, and
- ensuring that unitholder instructions are being correctly managed and executed.

In respect of the first bullet point, the manager of a CIS does not itself 'hold' the assets of the fund. The structure of collective investments requires an independent party (known as the depositary or trustee) to look after all scheme property on behalf of the unitholders of the fund. Therefore, even without the CASS 6 exemption we would recognise that the fund manager entity has no CASS responsibility for the fund's investment portfolio – because the manager is not performing a task of 'safeguarding and administration' in respect of those assets.

The position for unitholder activity is subtly different. Clearly the fund manager is receiving and executing orders from its clients (because a client will apply to the fund manager in order to buy or sell units in the fund). However, where the fund manager is acting in their capacity of fund manager, those unit deals are executed against the main register of the fund. Each client becomes a direct unitholder on the main register of the fund. No firm or intermediary is involved in a chain of custody; there is no nominee arrangement; the insolvency of the fund manager would not create a gap in the records relating to ownership of the units – because the main register of the fund (itself subject to specific FCA rules outside the scope of this workbook) includes the names and personal data of each unitholder.

However, there is the possibility that the legal entity acting as fund manager might also undertake additional types of financial services activity, and this is the point that the CASS exemption guidance seeks to address. The exemption confirms that where the firm is undertaking 'excluded custody activities', the custody rules do not apply. 'Excluded custody activities' essentially reflect any point at which the firm might be viewed as holding a custody position as a result of performing its duties as fund manager.

However, if the firm performs any types of business that are not directly associated with its regulatory obligations as fund manager (ie, business outside of receiving direct applications for main register activity), the CASS guidance confirms that the custody rules may still be applicable. CASS uses MiFID business as a simple example. When acting as fund manager, the firm is subject to UK rules applicable to fund managers (largely derived from the EU's UCITS and AIFM Directives). If however, the firm does offer a wider range of services outside the scope of its pure fund manager activity, then such additional services are likely to be subject to UK MiFID – in which case, the custody rules would be applicable to those services.

3.4   Delivery versus Payment (DvP) Transactions

3.4.1   What Does the Exemption Do?

CASS 6 includes an exemption for 'delivery versus payment' (DvP) transactions performed within a 'commercial settlement system'. Applying this exemption to a purchase or sale transaction performed for a client can allow the firm a window during which the asset need not be treated as a CASS 6 asset (the window lasts until the close of the third business day after the firm delivers its side of settlement). The exemption may avoid the creation of CASS 6 shortfalls if there are problems with market settlement of a transaction, thus removing the need for the firm to cover such positions. (It should be noted that there is a corresponding DvP exemption within CASS 7, such that the same window is available for both the asset being traded and the corresponding cash settlement sum.)

The fact that this DvP exemption is applied to both the asset and the associated cash settlement sum reflects that this exemption applies where a 'commercial settlement system' is used – and recognises that such systems may require the firm to part with either the asset or purchase consideration sum prior to the transaction settling. The FCA's objective of maintaining orderly markets means that CASS obligations should not create undue barriers to market liquidity. Accordingly, for certain firms in certain circumstances, the CASS rules allow firms to complete these trades without creating temporary shortfall positions that could require substantial amounts of corporate money to cover.

As using this exemption creates an exposure to client loss (if the firm was to fail before the settlement was fully completed, and an incoming insolvency practitioner was unable to achieve settlement of the transaction) there are some important requirements before it can be applied:

1. The client concerned must have provided written agreement confirming that the firm may apply the exemption.
2. The firm must intend to exchange the client's money for their asset within one business day of each other. (Note: the transaction should be expected to leave the client exposed for no longer than one day – though the exemption permits the firm up to close of business on the third business day following the commencement of its use of the exemption, if required to resolve any problems with achieving market settlement. If, however, the firm expects the transaction type would usually leave the client exposed for more than one day, the exemption should not be used.)
3. The firm must be a direct member or participant of the relevant commercial settlement system, or can be a sponsored member.
4. The transaction must be completed in accordance with the terms and conditions of the commercial settlement system.
5. The transaction must be settled directly by the firm in an account held at the commercial settlement system.

Once the firm has received the settlement proceeds of an asset sale or received the asset purchased for the client, it must stop using the exemption and apply the CASS 6 and CASS 7 rules in the normal way.

3.4.2   What is a DvP Transaction?

There is no specific FCA Handbook Glossary definition of DvP, and so firms will need to make their own determination as to how broadly this term might be applied – and be ready to justify their stance if their auditor seeks clarification.

Reflecting on our initial comments regarding legal contracts, every contract requires valuable consideration – so every trade involving the delivery of an asset by one party is expected to involve a corresponding payment by the other.

However, the comments included in CASS in respect of this exemption imply a context in which the design and operation of the commercial settlement system will create a gap in protection between the delivery of the asset and the corresponding cash settlement (or vice versa).

Each firm will, therefore, need to determine what types of activity it considers will be DvP transactions for the purposes of this exemption.

3.4.3   What is a Commercial Settlement System?

The exemption can also only be applied if the DvP transaction is being performed through a commercial settlement system. A commercial settlement system is defined in the FCA Handbook Glossary as follows:

> 'a system commercially available to firms that are members or participants, a purpose of which is to facilitate the settlement of transactions using money and/or assets held on one or more settlement accounts'.

A 'settlement account' is itself defined in the Handbook. In brief, the definition relates to an account holding money and/or assets, held with an institution acting as settlement agent and used to settle transactions between participants or members of that commercial settlement system.

A firm wishing to use this exemption should therefore satisfy itself that the trading/settlement mechanism in question satisfies the Handbook definitions.

3.5   Allocated but Unclaimed Safe Custody Assets

While not an 'exemption' as such, CASS 6 includes a process by which a firm holding unclaimed safe custody assets can dispose of the holding by making a payment to charity. The process is similar to the corresponding approach for unclaimed amounts of client money, though with some differences.

The two most significant differences are:

1. the safe custody asset must have been held for at least 12 years (rather than the six years required to dispose of a client money balance), and
2. there is no *de minimis* option – so when using the CASS rules to dispose of safe custody assets of any value, the full requirements of CASS must be satisfied.

The firm must demonstrate that it has taken 'reasonable steps' to trace the client concerned. The evidential provision describing such reasonable steps would be satisfied if the firm took the following approach:

*   Determine, as far as possible, the correct contact details for the client.
*   Write to the client – at their last known postal or electronic mail address advising that the asset will be disposed of if no instruction is received in the following 28 days.
*   If no response is received in those 28 days, attempt a further communication via a different method of communication.
*   If still no response is received after a further 28 days, write one final time to the client advising that the asset will be disposed of within 28 days.
*   If still no response is received, the firm can dispose of the asset.
*   The firm can either sell the asset and effect payment of the proceeds to a registered charity, or could potentially transfer ownership of the asset to a registered charity.

As with client money balances paid to charity, if the firm receives positive confirmation that none of the contact details for the client remain current, it is not obliged to effect further written communications.

If the firm does effect the payment to a registered charity, the firm must undertake to pay the client the value liquidated/transferred if the client should contact the firm at any point in the future.

Lastly, this approach applies only where the firm seeks to dispose of the asset without receiving an instruction from the client. There may be occasions where a client of the firm may receive a small number of residual shares – too small to trade efficiently – and instruct the firm to effect a payment to charity. The firm in such a situation would not be applying this process, but simply fulfilling the client's instructions.

Learning Objective

5.4.1 Understand the impact of legal arrangements on the custody rules (CASS 6): bare security interests; right to use clauses/rehypothecation; title transfer collateral arrangements (TTCA)

5.4.2 Understand when the collateral rules (CASS 3) apply

5.4.3 Understand when a firm can enter into securities financing transactions in respect of client assets

5.4.4 Know the circumstances in which liens may be granted over client assets

CASS 6 requires the firm to maintain any client safe custody asset as properly registered and subject to reconciliation controls. However, there are certain types of investment-related activity that a firm might agree to undertake for its client that would require the asset to be moved to a different firm.

The legal contract between firm and client will need to make clear whether the firm has any authority to remove assets from the protection of CASS 6 rules and we will explore different contexts for this.

First, we must understand what is meant by 'collateral' and when collateral might be used between regulated firms or between a regulated firm and its clients.

4.1 Collateral

Put simply, collateral is a means of mitigating the risk on a contract. So far, we have looked at financial services transactions that have a defined trade date and settlement date, generally only a few days apart. However, there are more complex types of financial services contracts that extend for longer periods and which can build up substantial financial exposures between the parties. One example is derivative trading (such as taking a position in financial futures, or taking part in a put or call option).

Where a deal is struck under which one party is obliged to effect future delivery of a given asset (or its corresponding value), it is common for the parties to agree that a portion of the outstanding value should be exchanged at the outset to mitigate the overall exposure.

It is important to note, therefore, that the collateral is not part of settling the deal; it is always the intention of the parties that collateral will remain the actual property of the original owner. However, in order to be effective as collateral it might need to be 'pledged' (set aside – which may include registering the asset to some independent party) or transferred to the counterparty (in which case both firms will maintain records of what collateral has passed between them, so that it can be returned once the contractual position between them has been closed out and the exposure therefore resolved).

If a firm agrees or offers to provide its clients with a means to perform such types of investment activity, it will be necessary for the firm to manage the related collateral movements with whatever other firm is acting as counterparty to the transactions. This raises a question: if collateral is to be provided, does the firm use its own money (or assets) to provide the collateral, or does it use its client's money (or assets)? A second question follows if the firm wishes to use client money or client safe custody assets as collateral: does CASS allow the firm to change the registration of the asset, or have that asset held by a different party?

In terms of CASS therefore, it is important to understand what flexibility may exist within the rules, so that such investment activity can be undertaken for clients – providing those clients understand the risks associated with such types of transaction.

4.2   Bare Securities Interests

The word 'interest' can have various meanings. To have an 'interest' in a security means to have some stake in the value of the asset in question. The phrase *'bare securities interest'* effectively means *'to have an interest in the securities, but nothing more'*. That may sound odd at first, but as we look at more complex legal arrangements the comment will make more sense.

Understanding when a bare securities interest could be established will also help understanding of the concept. Suppose a firm is running a service that includes providing custody of client safe custody assets. The firm will be charging a fee for this service, and expect its client to pay their bill. However, in case the client does not pay, the firm will generally include in its terms and conditions a right to sell some assets of the client in order to settle the sum owed. In other words, until any such debt becomes outstanding, the firm only has a bare interest in the securities – it is looking after the assets on behalf of its client, but has the ability to acquire or dispose of an asset in order to settle some amount due and payable to the firm.

Any such right must be set out in the client agreement defining the firm's services. In English law, it is known as a 'lien': a right granted over an asset to secure some future payment (or the fulfilment of some other type of obligation between the parties). In Scottish law (or countries having legal systems derived from Roman law), the term 'hypothec' may be used.

A key feature of a lien is that the asset remains the legal property of the first party until that first party fails to fulfil their obligations under the contract concerned – at which point, full ownership of the asset passes to the second party in settlement of that obligation. When granting a lien it is generally expected that the asset will at no point change hands, though the existence of the lien makes it easier for the parties to do business together, as the creditor's risk is mitigated at no effective cost to the debtor.

A bare security interest is not therefore an example of collateral, because the asset does not change owner unless the terms are triggered on a default. Creating the bare security interest does not itself require any transfer of ownership/registration; it only creates a legal understanding that if the debtor party defaults on its payment, the full ownership of the asset concerned would transfer to the creditor party. CASS 3 is not applicable to such cases, as the registration of the asset/money is unaffected while the lien is in place.

4.3   'Right to Use' Clauses

Slightly more complex are situations where the client might grant to the firm a 'right to use' some or all assets – and collateral is a good example. Suppose a client of Dependable Investments ltd (Dependable) wants to enter into a financial futures contract or stock lending arrangement – both of which would require Dependable to provide collateral to the relevant counterparty.

If Dependable wants to use the client's assets as collateral it must ensure that it obtains from its client a right to use that client's assets for that purpose. CASS 3 confirms that in such a case exercising the right to use an asset equates to a change in legal ownership of that asset, such that it belongs to the firm rather than the client. Such an event must be clearly recorded in the firm's books and records.

While the right to use may exist, any asset covered by such a right remains a normal client asset (subject to normal CASS controls and protections) until the right to use is exercised and the firm's records updated to reflect that change in legal ownership. Stock lending is a form of securities financing transaction (SFT), which is also subject to European SFT regulations. Other forms of SFT include margin lending transactions and repurchase transactions.

4.4   Rehypothecation

CASS does not refer to the term 'hypothecation' – though it is prudent to understand the risk that this technique may represent.

We have noted that taking collateral does change the legal ownership of an asset – and that the firm would require a 'right to use' clause in its client agreement if it is to use some client assets as collateral.

Rehypothecation is a term used in the industry to describe the ability of a regulated firm to itself then pledge that collateral asset in respect of some other business being undertaken by the regulated firm. The regulated firm is therefore able to back out its own financial exposures, but the danger to the industry is the potential that the same asset is effectively being used by multiple parties to cover multiple exposures. In the event that one regulated firm in such a chain of counterparties was to become insolvent, or for some other reason fail to make delivery of some asset, there can be knock-on implications for other firms who were also protecting their own positions with reference to that same asset.

Investigations into the collapse of Lehman Brothers and MF Global identified that rehypothecation was a contributing factor in the failure of those companies. Firms should recognise the risks involved in supporting their own financial positions with reference to assets that are not actually registered in their own name – as such assets might not be delivered to the firm if called upon.

4.5   Title Transfer Collateral Arrangements (TTCAs)

CASS 6 and CASS 7 give specific details about when and how title transfer collateral arrangements (TTCAs) can be effected, given the types of risks and exposures noted above.

A 'title transfer collateral arrangement' is defined in the FCA Handbook Glossary to mean any arrangement by which the client transfers full ownership of money or an asset to a firm for the purpose of securing or otherwise covering a present or future, actual, prospective, or contingent obligation.

The key legal consideration, and largest risk consideration for the client, is that once the firm has exercised the power of the TTCA to take ownership of the asset concerned, the asset from that point becomes the legal property of the firm and is no longer protected as a client asset. While the firm is under an obligation to return the asset to the client (subject to the terms of the TTCA), in the event that the firm subsequently fails, the client would only be able to claim against the firm as a general creditor – which offers less protection for that client, and is very likely to result in loss if the firm was to become insolvent.

CASS rules (as derived from MiFID) prohibit the firm from entering into a TTCA with a retail client. If a firm wishes to enter into a TTCA with another type of client, then the parties must enter into a formal contract (either in writing or some other durable medium, ie, some types of retrievable media confirming their agreement to the terms). The agreement should include the arrangements for transferring ownership to the firm, and any arrangements for subsequently returning the asset to the client's legal ownership.

The firm must be able to demonstrate that is has properly considered the appropriateness of operating a TTCA for the client concerned, in the light of the 'client's best interests' rule.

Let us briefly consider a TTCA in operation:

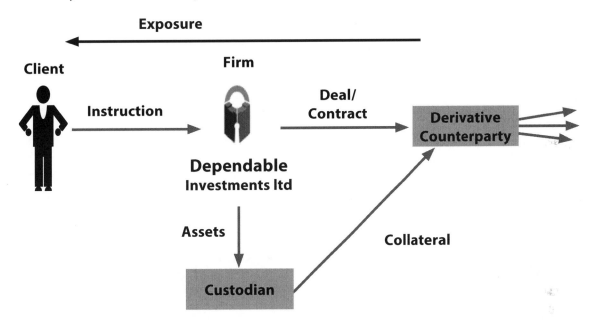

Dependable offers its clients an opportunity to take exposures under derivative contracts, which it secures with a derivative counterparty.

In order to maintain those exposures, Dependable may need to provide some asset collateral to the counterparty, which it achieves by first taking legal ownership of the client's asset under a TTCA.

Providing all parties achieve the eventual settlement of the derivative exposure, everyone will be satisfied: the collateral will be returned, the investor will receive the return on the derivative position, and Dependable will collect its servicing fees.

However, if the derivative counterparty was to fail, the position changes:

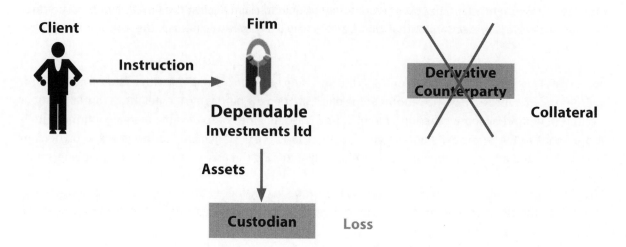

The contract between Dependable and the derivative counterparty fails, such that the client will now not receive any return from the derivative exposure. Further, the collateral that had been moved to the counterparty will be caught up in the insolvency of that entity, and so may not be returned to Dependable.

This creates an effective loss, as the custodian account holds less assets than was previously the case because the client gave Dependable a 'right to use' their assets as corporate assets in order to secure the derivative exposure.

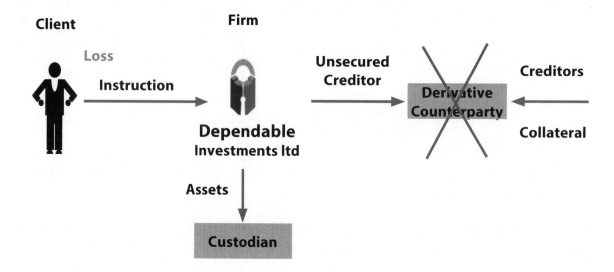

Dependable is simply an unsecured creditor of the failed counterparty, unlikely to recover the full value of the collateral transferred. As a result, the loss will effectively fall on the investor.

There would be a similar chain of events if Dependable was to fail, even if the derivative counterparty remained in operation.

End of Chapter Questions

Think of an answer for each question and refer to the appropriate section for confirmation

1. What regulated activities relate to safe custody assets?
   Answer reference: Section 2.1

2. What matters should a firm consider when performing due diligence on a third party to hold safe custody assets?
   Answer reference: Section 2

3. What is meant by an 'intragroup' safe custody model, and how does such a model affect due diligence obligations?
   Answer reference: Section 2

4. In what ways might CASS allow non-UK assets to be registered that would not be acceptable for UK assets?
   Answer reference: Section 2.2

5. What exemptions apply to the custody rules?
   Answer reference: Section 4

6. What is a bare security interest?
   Answer reference: Section 4.2

7. What is a 'right to use' and who would use this arrangement?
   Answer reference: Section 4.3

8. What is rehypothecation?
   Answer reference: Section 4.4

9. What is a title transfer collateral arrangement?
   Answer reference: Section 4.5

10. What risk arises for the client when a title transfer collateral arrangement (TTCA) is being used?
    Answer reference: Section 4.5

Chapter Six
Controls over Safe Custody Assets (CASS 6)

This syllabus area will provide approximately 5 of the 50 examination questions

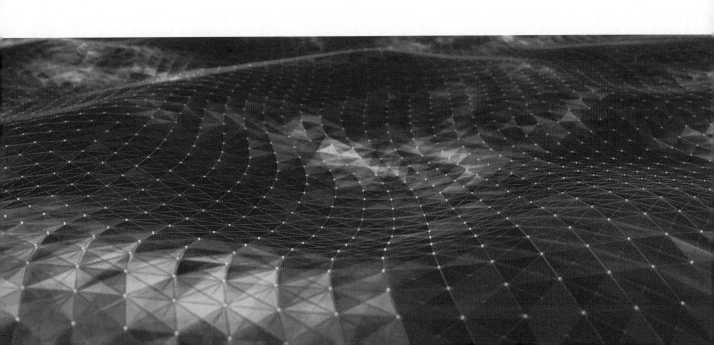

Introduction

In this chapter, we will explore the control processes that a firm must establish to ensure that its clients are protected from the risk of their safe custody assets being lost, or return delayed, in the event of the firm's insolvency. Again we will see parallels with the controls required to protect client money – with key components being the selection of relevant third parties, the records maintained by the firm, and a discipline of reconciling those records to ensure that discrepancies are identified and resolved.

1. Custody Books and Records

Learning Objective

6.1.1 Know which books and records should be maintained and the function of each

It is important that the firm maintains an accurate and complete record of which of its clients has ownership rights for which of the safe custody assets held by the firm. Recording the entitlement of each client is therefore vital (ie, the vostro record). However, unlike the obligation in CASS 7 for the firm to maintain a distinct record of its aggregated bank account, CASS 6 does not require the firm to have a separate ledger of its aggregated holdings. While the firm may choose to maintain such a distinct ledger, it is sufficient under CASS 6 for the firm to determine its aggregated client safe custody position as the calculated sum of all client-specific asset balances.

It should be noted that the firm's custody records should reflect the aggregate safe custody assets actually held by the firm, rather than assets to be received at a future settlement date. The firm's records of client entitlement to assets will reflect the assets that the firm contractually considers belong to the client (which may reflect contractual settlement of assets not yet held in the firm's aggregate position) in the market. We will see in the following section what actions a firm will be required to take if its reconciliation between these different records identifies that insufficient or excess assets are held.

Controls over pending inflight transactions are important to successful settlement processes, and so while firms are likely to implement a range of controls it is important that the firm's records recognise 'held' assets:

- Cash records reflect the cash positions that are 'held' by the firm.
- Settlement date is the point at which assets bought become 'held' by the firm in exchange for it no longer holding cash. While cash might be reserved in the firm's records between trade date and settlement date, the money remains client money (or a deposit for firms utilising the banking exemption) until completion and the corresponding discharge of fiduciary duty.

2.1 Safe Custody Asset Reconciliations and Checks

Learning Objective

6.2.1 Understand the purpose of the external custody reconciliations, physical asset reconciliations, and internal custody record checks

There are three types of record check (or equivalent) that can arise in respect of client safe custody assets, though some firms will not need to perform all three types. These are:

- external custody reconciliation
- physical asset reconciliation
- internal custody record check (ICRC).

CASS includes guidance stating that, wherever possible, these checks and reconciliations should be carried out by employees that are independent, ie, people who are not involved in producing or maintaining the records being checked.

The external custody reconciliation is broadly similar to the external client money reconciliation:

- the firm determines from its own record the total amount of each asset held for its clients (whether calculated from client entitlements or taken from a discrete record of the firm's aggregated position)
- the firm compares this figure against the amount of each asset that the external custodian or other third party states is held on the firm's behalf.

CASS requires a firm to undertake this reconciliation 'as regularly as necessary', though the period between external custody reconciliations must not exceed one month.

Similarly, the physical asset reconciliation is only relevant to firms that hold physical assets on behalf of their customers. The context here is a vault room, filled with filing cabinets holding physical items (such as share certificates). We have already shown that the firm must keep a record of each client's entitlement to the assets held, and so the physical asset reconciliation is required to ensure that the assets which should be held in the vault are present and correct.

CASS offers two methods that a firm can use when performing a physical asset reconciliation, as explained in the following table. It is perhaps useful to imagine the practical challenge of reconciling a large inventory of physical assets, in order to understand the need for these two different methods.

Method	How the method works
Total Count Method	The reconciliation is performed as a single check – effectively the person(s) performing the reconciliation would start with the first certificate, typically alphabetically, and work through to the last until complete over a defined period, often over a weekend.

Such an approach seems sensible providing it can be achieved logistically because any misfiled assets should be identified as part of the single reconciliation effort undertaken. |
| Rolling Stock Method | A firm might instead perform the reconciliation in stages (either through choice or because it is not logistically possible to complete the physical count in a single sitting). The first day of the reconciliation might complete all assets beginning with the letter 'A'; the second day of reconciliation activity (perhaps on the following weekend) might review the assets beginning with 'B'. Under the rolling stock method, the firm works its way methodically through the entire inventory in as many sittings as are necessary to promptly complete the reconciliation. |

Whichever method is selected, CASS requires that the physical asset reconciliation be performed as regularly as necessary – but without more than six months passing between each reconciliation.

At first it might appear that the rolling stock method is inferior to the total count method, because a lost or misfiled item seems to take longer to find under the rolling stock method. Indeed, CASS rules require a firm that adopts the rolling stock method to document that its methodology is '…adequately designed to mitigate the risk of the firm's records being manipulated or falsified'. However, as both methods are subject to a six-month maximum frequency, it might equally be considered that either method could result in a lost or misfiled item not being identified for up to six months from that error taking place.

The firm must make its own decision as to what frequency it considers to be 'as regularly as necessary' (subject to the maximum six-month period). That decision must be documented as a policy of the firm, and the firm should perform an annual review to ensure that its policy decision remains appropriate in light of its current service model and any issues experienced. The firm should also ensure that the reconciliations are performed by individuals who are independent of the operational processes being validated.

Physical stocks are not required and indeed could not be included in external reconciliations, although sample spot checks to registrar's records are recommended.

2.2 Internal Custody Record Check (ICRC)

Note that this is a 'record check' rather than a 'reconciliation'. This reflects the point noted above that CASS 6 does not require a firm to maintain an internal record of its aggregate safe custody asset positions separate from its client-level records. For this reason, CASS identifies two ways in which the internal custody record check might be achieved. In either case, CASS requires the firm to complete an ICRC '...*as regularly as necessary*...' but without allowing more than one month to elapse between each ICRC. Again, this is a policy decision that must be documented and subject to annual review. Staff performing the ICRC should again be independent of the functions being reviewed.

Method	How the method works
Internal Custody Reconciliation Method	Where a firm's systems are designed so that it does maintain two distinct asset records – one tracking each client's entitlement, and a separate record tracking the firm's aggregated holding for its clients – then the ICRC can be achieved by performing a formal reconciliation between these two distinct internal records.
Internal System Evaluation Method (ISEM)	Where a firm's systems do not separately determine the aggregate asset position, performing such a reconciliation would be meaningless. In such a case, the firm must use the internal system evaluation method (ISEM) to complete the ICRC (though ISEM can be selected by any firm – even one that does maintain distinct asset ledgers). ISEM requires the firm to consider its own system and data structure, and to identify those scenarios and actions that pose a risk to the accurate recording of the trades executed by the firm. For this reason, the CASS material on ISEM is understandably generic, as ISEM requires each firm to first determine for itself those controls that are fundamental to the accuracy of its client-level custody records. The ISEM itself is a periodic internal review carried out so that the firm can satisfy itself that those controls have been working as designed, and that any exception items identified have been investigated and resolved as planned. In this way, it should detect certain types of weakness and record-keeping discrepancies.

A firm adopting ISEM must establish a process that evaluates the completeness and accuracy of its internal records. That evaluation should include whether the firm's fundamental CASS 6 controls have correctly identified and resolved discrepancies in the firm's internal records of safe custody assets. CASS provides a non-exhaustive list of items that the firm should consider when devising their ISEM:

- negative balances
- processing errors
- journal entry errors
- IT errors, and
- 'test' entries or 'balancing' entries that might incorrectly over/understate the size of a holding.

The firm must consider what behaviours its systems should exhibit, and what controls should prevent other behaviours arising, and then the ISEM evaluates whether those controls have been effective.

While it is true that the FCA has therefore not defined the detailed completion of an ISEM, it is important to note that ISEM is a process to evaluate whether the firm's controls have effectively identified and resolved errors within its internal record of safe custody assets held for its clients. However, as we saw when considering CASS 7 controls, the controls established over the firm's CASS 6 records (including its Internal Custody Reconciliation, or an ISEM established to evaluate the controls) should not be expected to prevent all forms of potential error. Where a firm might have made an error when executing a given transaction (such as buying the wrong asset), the firm's internal custody record should reflect the actual trade executed. Therefore, ISEM need not be expected to identify errors in the execution of trades; such errors fall within the remit of Conduct of Business Sourcebook (COBS) regulations rather than CASS. CASS becomes important once the firm has executed a transaction – to ensure that the assets (and money) actually held by the firm in light of the executed activity are correctly segregated and protected.

Of course, as each firm that has a custody responsibility for assets is obliged to perform these reconciliations and checks, it follows that the same checks are being performed by each UK-regulated firm along a custody chain. The following illustrates the scenario where clients transact via a platform, which holds an account at a third-party custody account in the name of its nominee company, and the custodian has an aggregated holding on the asset's main register:

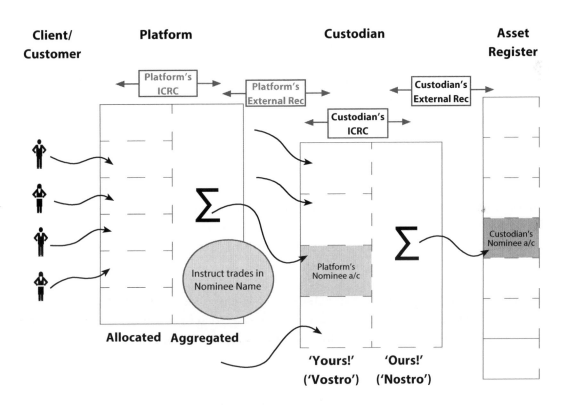

The platform must perform its ICRC (which might be the internal reconciliation method, if the firm has a separate aggregate holdings ledger) and an external custody reconciliation. The custodian will similarly be performing internal and external checks and reconciliations, and so on back to the end of the custody chain.

2.3   Reconciliation Discrepancies

Learning Objective

6.2.2   Understand how to treat reconciliation discrepancies

6.2.3   Understand firms' obligations in relation to shortfalls

Any discrepancy identified in any of these reconciliations or ICRC processes should be promptly investigated and resolved. Resolution here may, however, be a longer process than the resolution stages we discussed for cash, because the firm may not simply be able to deliver additional shares. The firm may need to place a market trade to make up any difference identified.

Suppose a firm's internal records showed that its clients had a beneficial interest in 35,000 Marks & Spencer (M&S) plc shares, while the firm's custodian reports that it holds only 30,000 M&S shares for the firm. The firm's external custody reconciliation will identify a shortfall of 5,000 shares – and if the firm believes it is responsible for that shortfall it must consider what remediation is required.

If the firm is a large institution that also trades on its own account, it may well have a separate portfolio that holds 5,000 M&S shares. If so, the firm could simply transfer the necessary shares from its own corporate asset account to its client safe custody asset account. This would bring swift resolution of the client asset shortfall – and this is achieved by the firm putting its own assets into the client account to resolve the discrepancy (in the same way that corporate money is used to resolve a client money reconciliation discrepancy).

However, suppose the firm does not hold its own investment portfolio. Buying the 'missing' 5,000 shares will require it to place a deal with a broker, which will only settle in two days' time (potentially longer for other asset types). In such a case, CASS requires the firm to segregate sufficient cash or other assets to cover the shortfall position. If the firm does place a market transaction to buy the necessary shares, then it can treat the shortfall by segregating the relevant sum of corporate money to settle that future market obligation. Such a cash figure remains fixed until settlement date, as the cost of buying the 'missing' shares has been fixed by the trade executed in the market.

The firm might however decide to not purchase the missing shares, and to instead cover the asset shortfall using either cash and/or some other corporate asset held by the firm. In such a case, the firm would be obliged to ensure each day that the value of cash and/or assets it has segregated against the shortfall remains sufficient against the current value of the missing 5,000 shares. The value must be determined by the previous day's closing mark to market valuation.

CASS recognises that the firm might not be to blame for a shortfall arising. If the firm's investigations conclude that the discrepancy is the fault of some other person, the firm must take all reasonable steps to seek resolution of the problem by that other party. In the meantime, the firm should however still consider whether to notify the affected client and/or fund any shortfall that has arisen. The only exception is where the firm considers that a shortfall has arisen only because the records used to perform the reconciliation have been produced at different times (such as where a firm in the UK is reconciling its UK close of business position against a custodian account with a US-based institution).

2.4 Establishing the Frequency of Safe Custody Reconciliations and Checks

Learning Objective

6.2.4   Know how often the reconciliations must be carried out

When discussing each of the safe custody checks and reconciliations we saw that, while CASS specifies a maximum period between checks, the firm must ensure that the task is performed '...*as regularly as necessary...*'.

CASS requires the firm to consider the nature of the CASS activity in order to determine a suitable frequency for performing these checks, and consider how these would affect the records being maintained. The firm should consider the transactions it undertakes: does it trade a high volume of deals? Are those deals for high value? The firm should also consider whether the transactions expose its clients to a greater risk, assessed in respect of the nature, volume and complexity of those transactions (eg, does the firm enable derivative transactions or short-selling, which could affect the extent of potential loss if an error was identified after a longer period).

Having concluded this analysis, the firm should formally document the frequency with which it will perform the internal custody record check, external custody reconciliation, and physical asset reconciliation, and these chosen frequencies should be reviewed at least annually to ensure that the decisions remain appropriate in the light of any change in the firm's business model or activities.

End of Chapter Questions

Think of an answer for each question and refer to the appropriate section for confirmation

1.   What records and accounts must a firm maintain on safe custody assets?
     Answer reference: Section 1

2.   Aside from the internal custody record check (ICRC), CASS 6 describes two types of
     reconciliation. What are these reconciliations and to what do they relate?
     Answer reference: Section 2.1

3.   What are the two methods of internal custody record check (ICRC)?
     Answer reference: Section 2.3

4.   Where a firm uses the internal system evaluation method (ISEM), what five elements does CASS 6
     require a firm to include in the design of the ISEM?
     Answer reference: Section 2.3

5.   What is the process for discrepancies and shortfalls?
     Answer reference: Section 2.4

Chapter Seven

Governance and Oversight

This syllabus area will provide approximately 6 of the 50 examination questions

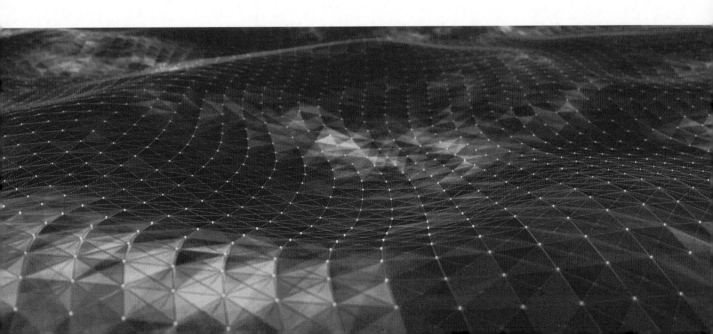

Introduction

We have now explored the specific controls that CASS requires a firm to have put in place to mitigate the risk of loss when handling and controlling client money and safe custody assets.

However, we have also seen that CASS grants firms a substantial amount of flexibility in the ways that they structure their business processes. It is, therefore, important that the firm has a holistic understanding of where those structural choices could expose its clients to risk, and ensures that sufficient and appropriate mitigation is in place to manage those risks.

In particular, this chapter will focus on four broad areas:

- CASS rules regarding the firm's 'organisational arrangements'
- the individual who is responsible for CASS oversight
- the need for the firm to exercise good corporate governance, including oversight of any operational outsourcing in place
- the CASS audit performed on the firm.

1. Organisational Arrangements

1.1 CASS Rules in respect of 'Organisational Arrangements'

Learning Objective

7.1.1 Know the rules on organisational arrangements as set out in CASS 6 and CASS 7

7.1.2 Know firms' obligations to notify the FCA of breaches in accordance with CASS 6 and 7

Both CASS 6 and CASS 7 include a high-level statement taken from the Markets in Financial Instruments Directive (MiFID). The CASS 7 wording requires the firm to '...*make adequate arrangements...*' to safeguard client rights, and to '...*introduce adequate organisational arrangements to minimise the risk of the loss of diminution of client money...*' as a result of factors such as misuse, fraud, poor administration, or inadequate record-keeping. — *Keep it safe.*

The CASS 6 wording is similar, requiring the firm to have '...*adequate organisational arrangements to minimise the risk of loss or diminution of clients' safe custody assets...*' due to similar underlying causes.

A key observation here is that these words do not require perfection; risk will remain in any business model – but the firm should be able to demonstrate in a coherent and holistic manner that the array of processes and controls in place are adequate to minimise the risk of loss of clients' assets.

Interpretation and application of such rules can be a challenge – and it should be recognised that this MiFID wording reflects a European legal perspective (which emphasises the intended outcomes, while English law tends to consider detailed aspects of all potential outcomes).

Consider the case of an internal client money reconciliation. The specific CASS rules require the firm to identify any incorrect postings in that reconciliation and correct any resulting shortfall or excess. The specific rules consider it sufficient for such identification and resolution to be achieved on the date the reconciliation is performed.

Some would therefore argue that the wording of broad organisation requirements should not be interpreted as needing any more stringent a requirement in respect of identification and resolution of shortfall/excess sums. If the EU rules had demanded something stronger, the drafting would have applied additional obligations.

Some in the industry have taken the opposite interpretation, and argued that any failing arising in client money control indicates a failure of organisational arrangements.

The key is for the firm to understand where risk can arise, whether that risk is due to internal causes or external factors, and understand whether any decisions taken by the firm in arranging its business could present risk exposure that is unreasonable in context.

It should also be noted that the organisational arrangements rules relate to overall structures, rather than to specific cases of operational error. An operational error does not mean that the firm's overall organisational arrangements are flawed. Equally, where the firm's organisational arrangements are flawed, that position exists regardless of whether any specific operational incident occurs as a result of that weakness, ie, it is not a defence to claim that despite being flawed, controls are sufficient because the firm by luck did not experience a breach.

Therefore, any firm that determines itself to be in breach of the organisational arrangements rule would need to identify some way of amending those arrangements in order to close the associated breach.

CASS 7 includes some Financial Conduct Authority (FCA) guidance on the application of the MiFID requirement. One example it references is the clearance period associated with money that the firm might receive via different payment methods. The key point is that the firm must consider the active consequences of the payment methods it supports; consider when ledger postings ought to be generated in order to most correctly reflect the client money position; and ensure that the overall business model represents in its view an adequate management of the risks inherent in investment transactions and settlement activity.

1.2 FCA Notifiable Breaches

There is therefore a strong connection between the firm's satisfaction with its organisational arrangements and any CASS breaches that may have arisen, as root-cause analysis of these breaches may suggest a systemic weakness rather than an isolated human error.

However, in addition to the natural use of breach data to help a firm reduce the risk of further errors, CASS 6 and CASS 7 each contain a list of breaches or failures which, if they arise, must be immediately notified to the FCA. These are events of significance, which the FCA considers could be indicative of a firm that may be experiencing serious difficulties in achieving the required client asset protections. Requiring the firm to formally notify the FCA that such a breach has arisen would enable the regulator to become involved prior to any actual business failure taking place.

CASS contains two separate lists of notification requirements (one in CASS 6 and another in CASS 7). While both lists cover essentially the same types of risks and controls, we will list them separately for ease of reference:

CASS 6 requires a firm to notify the FCA if:

- its internal records and accounts of safe custody assets are materially out of date, or materially inaccurate/invalid, to the extent that the firm cannot distinguish assets held for different clients
- it is unable to (or materially fails to) take necessary steps relating to shortfall
- it is unable to (or materially fails to) conduct an internal custody record check (ICRC) at the frequency decided in the firm's policy
- it is unable to (or materially fails to) conduct a physical asset reconciliation at the frequency decided in the firm's policy
- it is unable to (or materially fails to) conduct an external custody reconciliation at the frequency decided in the firm's policy
- when acting as trustee/depositary of an alternative investment fund (AIF) or undertakings for collective investment in transferable securities (UCITS), the firm fails to distinguish safe custody assets held for one client from another client and from the firm's own applicable assets.

CASS 7 requires a firm to notify the FCA if:

- its internal records/accounts are materially out of date/inaccurate/invalid, to the extent that the firm cannot distinguish client money held for different clients
- it is unable to (or materially fails to) identify and resolve discrepancies having completed an external reconciliation
- it is unable to (or materially fails to) complete the daily internal client money reconciliation
- having completed the internal client money reconciliation, it is unable to (or materially fails to) resolve an identified shortfall or withdraw an identified excess
- it is unable to (or materially fails to) perform its external client money reconciliation as per the firm's internal policy
- it becomes aware that during the past 12 months the amount of client money actually segregated was materially different from the amount required to be segregated.

2. CASS Oversight within a Regulated Firm

Learning Objective

7.2.1 Understand the role responsible for CASS operational oversight within a firm, and its relationship with Prescribed Responsibility 'z'

In chapter 2, we noted that each regulated firm having permissions relating to client assets will be categorised as either a CASS large firm, CASS medium firm, or CASS small firm. We also noted that the FCA had created a specific senior management prescribed responsibility for CASS matters within the firm (prescribed responsibility 'z').

However, aside from this prescribed responsibility (which should reside with the most senior member of the firm's executive having responsibility for CASS), the CASS rules create a requirement for a 'director or senior manager' to have specific responsibility for overseeing the operational CASS model of the firm – and highlighting internally any concerns arising.

Within a CASS medium firm and CASS large firm this function has three key elements:

1. oversight of the operational effectiveness of the firm's systems and controls designed to achieve compliance with CASS
2. reporting to the firm's governing body in respect of that oversight, and
3. completing and submitting to the FCA a standard client money and assets return (CMAR).

While this individual need not be part of the executive management of the firm, they should be reportable to either a member of the Board or the head of a significant business unit. In some firms, this CASS oversight role will be allocated to the same individual holding prescribed responsibility 'z' – though in other firms separate people may be given these distinct responsibilities (with the prescribed responsibility 'z' given to the more senior within the company). *z for senior, specific oversight the CASS man*

A CASS small firm faces a broadly similar requirement, as it must allocate to a director or senior manager responsibility for two elements:

1. oversight of the firm's operational compliance with CASS, and *no CMAR for small*
2. reporting to the firm's governing body in respect of that oversight.

Note that in this case there is no requirement for the individual to complete and submit the CMAR, as a CASS small firm is not required to submit CMARs to the FCA.

We will now consider how this individual (sometimes referred to as the 'Client Assets Oversight Officer' or 'CAOO') will fulfil this responsibility.

2.1   Oversight of Operational Effectiveness

Throughout the workbook we have noted the importance of the firm recognising how its processes and procedures together enable client assets to be protected, and the range of approaches that a firm might take to its business structure while still providing the necessary protection. We have also noted how certain controls are specified within CASS, while other controls will need to be determined by the firm in light of the structures and process decisions it has taken. *understand business structure/model → oversight mechanism for CASS.*

The CAOO must understand this overall structure and the various decisions that have been taken in building the firm's business model. Armed with this understanding, they must devise an oversight mechanism that will demonstrate that the necessary systems and controls are in place to ensure that the firm's particular business model will successfully deliver effective compliance with CASS.

The larger the firm, or the more diverse its activities, the more complex the business model becomes and the more complex the CAOO's oversight activity will become. Larger organisations may outsource significant administrative functions to external service providers – potentially having multiple service providers, each supporting a different element of the overall business model. *Can outsource*

126

The CAOO is therefore likely to require regular reporting, from internal departments or outsourced service providers, to confirm that the operational procedures are being performed as expected. Any service disruptions having the potential to disrupt CASS processes should be communicated to the CAOO, and they are likely to seek management information about any CASS-related breaches that may have arisen – in particular to understand any control weaknesses indicated by the root-cause analysis.

The CAOO must therefore be thoughtful when drawing up the oversight approach, as it will always be possible to seek more information. Part of the skill in their role is to ensure that they obtain the right data to undertake the necessary analysis without being buried in excess information.

Expectation to analyse broad data

2.2 Reporting to the Firm's Governing Body

The CASS rules do not specify details as to how such reporting might be presented; the individual must determine what reporting should be provided to the governing body to ensure that it is sufficiently aware of any risks to overall continued CASS compliance. *No set structure so report*

The content and frequency of this reporting is therefore likely to reflect the nature, scale, and complexity of the firm's CASS affairs – and may be increased if a particular problem or concern is under review.

As with all controlled functions, the individual is personally responsible to the FCA for their proper conduct in fulfilling their function. The CAOO must therefore be confident that the reporting they provide to the governing body would be sufficient to satisfy the FCA if the regulator was to review the materials. Where prescribed responsibility 'z' is held by a different individual within the firm, that person will have a direct interest in the board-level discussions of the firm's CASS affairs.

2.3 Completion and Submission of Client Money and Assets Return (CMAR)

Learning Objective

7.2.2 Know the requirements for the content and submission of the Client Money and Assets Return (CMAR)

The CMAR is a formal periodic submission by the firm to the FCA as its regulator. The requirements of the report are therefore contained within the Supervision Sourcebook (SUP) rather than in the CASS Sourcebook. Note that a CASS small firm is not required to submit a CMAR.

Each CASS large firm and CASS medium firm must submit a CMAR each month. The data should be taken from the firm's internal records, effectively based on the close of business position as at the end of the calendar month (though firms need only submit the return by the 15th business day of the month). Therefore, the firm's internal reconciliation material completed on the first business day of each month is the primary source material for populating the CMAR.

The following table provides some information on the nine key elements that make up a CMAR:

No.	Element	Comment
1	Information about the firm	Core factual information: the firm's name; whether it held client money and/or safe custody assets during the month; whether the alternative approach to segregation was operated (and, if so, confirmation that the FCA had been made aware and the auditor had provided the necessary reports). This section also includes a summary of the firm's business activities – such as the type and number of clients serviced, and the balances/ value of client money and safe custody assets held at the end of the month.
2	High/low balances	The firm must confirm both the highest and lowest balances held during the month for both client money and safe custody assets (again, as shown in its internal records).
3	Client money segregation structure	The firm must provide information regarding each institution used to hold client money: name of the institution; the type of institution (for example, CRD credit institution, exchange or qualifying money market funds (QMMF)); the balance held; the country of incorporation; and whether it is a group entity of the firm.
4	Resource and requirement	Confirmation of the resource and requirement figures determined for the firm within the internal client money reconciliation performed on the first day of the month ended (ie, the figures as at close of business at the end of the month). The CMAR must confirm a number of the individual component amounts of the requirement calculation: unallocated but identified client money; uncleared payments; prudent segregation in place; any shortfall/excess identified; and any adjustments made as a result of the reconciliation.
5	Client money reconciliations	Confirmation of the firm's approach – including the frequency with which the firm performs internal and external client money reconciliations, and the number of unresolved client money reconciliation items recorded (split according to the age of the exception item: 6–29 days/30–59 days/60–90 days/90 days or longer).
6	Segregation of safe custody assets	High-level values, grouped according to registration method: how the assets are registered; how they are held; the name of the institution holding the assets; the number of stock lines registered in that way with that institution; the country of incorporation of the institution; and whether that institution is a group entity of the firm.
7	Safe custody asset record checks and reconciliations	The number of unresolved items remaining in the firm's reconciliations/record checks (split by age: 30–59 days/60–89 days/ over 90 days); confirmation of the frequency with which the firm performs each of the distinct safe custody asset reconciliations and record checks; and the types of assets included in each of those types of reconciliation/record check.

No.	Element	Comment
8	Record-keeping and breaches	Recording separately for client bank accounts (CBAs) and client transaction accounts (CTAs): the number of accounts open at the start and end of the month; the number opened or closed; the number with acknowledgement letters; and explanation where these numbers do not match. _→ ◇ Abut accounts_ The breach data reflects the number of notifiable breaches occurring, and confirmation that notification to the FCA was completed.
9	Outsourcing and offshoring	Each service provider is identified, stating the location, the CASS functions outsourced to that entity, and whether any significant changes are made or being planned. _to All third parties._

3. Corporate Governance Arrangements

3.1 Internal Corporate Governance Arrangements

Learning Objective

7.3.1 Understand the elements of good oversight, including appropriate governance, training, compliance, risk management, and internal audit

Aside from the specific obligations of the two specific senior CASS roles, each regulated firm should establish a range of corporate governance controls to ensure good oversight of its own activity.

Key corporate committees involved in directing the firm should have defined terms of reference; key management responsibilities should be allocated to staff of sufficient seniority, and staff should be given sufficient initial and ongoing training to ensure they are able to fulfil their duties correctly.

Such activity and controls are then supported and supplemented by certain independent functions within the company – risk management, compliance, and internal audit. Where the firm is subject to UK MiFID, the FCA Handbook reflects certain obligations, though any firm should consider the value of deploying specialists to act in these disciplines for the overall health of the firm.

3.1.1 Risk Management

The risk management function has responsibility for ensuring that the risks inherent in the firm's business activities are understood, and that appropriate mitigations are in place to reduce the residual risk exposure of the firm. Such risks would include the following:

- **Operational risks** – for example, any manual data input to the firm's systems or ledgers carries a risk of manual error. *Doing (people)*
- **Systems risks** – if automated systems become unavailable or corrupt, the firm may be unable to rely upon reporting or process outputs – potentially destabilising the firm's activities. Requirements of data protection are often linked to systems risks. *IT*
- **Counterparty risks** – where the firm's business is dependent upon the successful delivery of assets by market counterparties, the risk of failed delivery could have an impact on the firm's financial liquidity.
- **Vendor risks** – failure by any third party to deliver the services required could have a significant impact upon the firm's ability to fulfil its business obligations.

The risk management function will generally work to ensure an understanding of such matters within a structured framework to support the firm's governing body in making decisions to sufficiently mitigate these risks in a pragmatic and business-focused manner.

3.1.2   Compliance

The compliance function is responsible for understanding the regulatory obligations of the firm – whether in respect of its client-facing activity (such as providing information to clients), market-facing activity (settling transactions), or regulatory relationship (obligations applicable to the firm by virtue of it being a regulated firm – such as periodic reporting to the FCA).

The compliance function will support the firm in determining what is required for the firm to demonstrate compliance with the rules, and advise the operational areas accordingly. Compliance personnel should be available to support operational staff if any issues arise – to help prioritise remediation actions in line with relative regulatory expectations.

It will also perform internal compliance monitoring activity; a structured programme of sample-based reviews to demonstrate that the firm's procedures are (a) sufficient to demonstrate compliance with applicable rules; and (b) being correctly implemented by the operational areas concerned. Compliance and risk management functions are often referred to as the firm's 'second line of defence'. These 'second line' functions will generally deliver reviews of all corporate activity within a fixed review period (such as a year or 18 months).

3.1.3   Internal Audit

Internal audit is a broader discipline, and some smaller firms may not retain such a function. Like the 'second line' functions, internal audit will take a view over the firm's overall activity, ensuring that the firm's activities are efficient and controlled. The internal audit function is sometimes referred to as the 'third line of defence', as its own review programme will tend to focus on specific areas of concern, rather than seeking to replicate the 'second line' functions in reviewing all activities each year. Internal audit work tends to have a more intrusive focus, digging deeper into the underlying processes of the firm in order to draw out potential enhancements to improve delivery or efficiency.

3.2 Oversight of Outsourcing Arrangements

Learning Objective

7.3.2 Understand the firm's oversight responsibilities in respect of outsourcing arrangements

Outsourcing is any arrangement by which a regulated firm retains the services of another entity to perform administrative or other duties that would otherwise be performed by the firm itself. Importantly, a firm that outsources activity remains fully responsible under regulations for the correct performance of the tasks being performed on its behalf. Outsourcing is generally performed in the background, and the customers of the firm may for practical purposes not be aware if they are communicating with the firm itself or some outsourced service provider acting on behalf of the firm and in the firm's name.

Outsourcing is therefore different from the situation where one firm appoints another entity – such as a bank or a custodian – which is itself regulated and will be performing its own regulated activity in its own name. If we consider the custodian, for example, the firm will need to access the records of what assets and/or money the custodian shows as being held for the firm's nominee within the custody account – but the firm has no obligation to explore the custodian's nostro account (as this reflects the interior functioning of the custodian in performing its own regulated activity – which is not the responsibility of the firm). Similarly, the firm needs to access the account records maintained by its bank, but does not need to examine the internal workings of the bank's clearing processes. Such matters relate directly to the authorised activity of the bank or custodian concerned, and are not 'outsourcing' by the firm.

It is therefore important that the firm fully understands the tasks it has outsourced, in order that it can establish sufficient oversight of the performance of those tasks. Even though the outsourced service provider may not itself be regulated it will generally establish risk management controls and/or perform internal monitoring to ensure the accuracy of its work – and may provide certain outputs of such monitoring work to the firm.

However, the firm remains responsible for the actions of its outsourced service provider, so will generally require certain reporting – generally referred to as 'key performance indicators' (KPIs) – to give statistical information about the quality of service being received.

In addition, the firm will generally perform direct monitoring of the outsourced service provider – either using remote system access, or physical visits to the service provider's premises – to review the processing environment and validate the understanding and accuracy of work being performed.

It should of course be noted that the firm should be performing similar oversight of all work being undertaken within its own internal departments – but the fact that outsourcing involves a separate legal entity means that the firm must ensure it has the necessary access and expertise to perform the oversight it deems necessary.

One final observation regarding outsourcing: within some larger financial organisations a number of group legal entities may all outsource certain administrative functions to a single group company. Such 'intragroup' outsourcing raises the same regulatory obligations for oversight. However, there have been circumstances in the past where regulators have found that intragroup outsourcing arrangements have failed to sufficiently distinguish the records and accounts between the various group entities being serviced – such that insolvency of any one legal entity could have become unmanageable.

It is therefore important that all firms ensure that the records and accounts being maintained on their behalf are clear and distinct – whether they are created and maintained in-house, under an intragroup outsourcing arrangement, or by an external outsourced service provider. When outsourcing, it is particularly important to ensure that the records are maintained for each distinct legal entity being serviced.

again, responsible so work need to be accurate.

4. The CASS Audit

Learning Objective

7.4.1 Know the duty of the CASS auditor to submit a client assets report

7.4.2 Know the difference between a reasonable assurance engagement and a limited assurance engagement and when these apply

7.4.3 Know the content, format, and submission deadline of the client assets report and be aware of the FRC standard that applies

7.4.4 Know the role of the Financial Reporting Council (FRC) in respect of the client asset assurance standard

4.1 The Need for a CASS Audit

All companies have an auditor to ensure that their financial affairs are being correctly managed, and confirm the content of their company accounts, known as a statutory audit. In a similar way, the SUP Sourcebook requires many regulated firms to retain an auditor to ensure their CASS affairs are being correctly managed. *Separate to normal audit.*

We have already seen that the CASS auditor is required to give a formal opinion if the firm makes certain decisions regarding their CASS models – such as a decision to apply the 'alternative approach' to client money segregation. The annual CASS auditor's report is a separate, annual obligation.

The firm must appoint an auditor who is independent of the firm, and confirm to the FCA that an appointment has been made. The firm must then provide the auditor with the necessary access to accounting records and personnel – including any materials and personnel relating to outsourced services.

The CASS auditor is then directly responsible under SUP 3.10 to provide a client assets report to the FCA. Two different types of report can be produced: *— OK? Yes/No*

- **reasonable assurance engagement report** (used in most cases, where the CASS auditor has performed checks to validate the appropriateness of the firm's CASS processes), or
- **limited assurance engagement report** (used where the firm is obliged to have a report produced, but claims that it held no client assets during the period).

Both of these types of report follow the FCA rules in SUP 3.10 and are also governed by standards defined by the Financial Reporting Council (FRC) (effectively the trade body for auditors, therefore responsible for ensuring a consistent standard of CASS audit activity across the country). The FRC's Client Asset Assurance Standard is periodically updated, with the most recent change being implemented for accounting periods beginning from 1 January 2020. As the auditor is responsible for ensuring that the audit is carried out in accordance with the standard, firms should seek to understand any proposed changes to the FRC standard in order to ensure that the relevant information can be made available to their auditors once that revised standard becomes effective.

Each CASS audit must cover a period of no longer than 53 weeks, beginning from either the previous CASS audit or the date of the firm becoming authorised and subject to the CASS audit requirement. The report must be submitted to the FCA within four months after the end of the period. For this reason, it is common for the auditor to perform some testing over the course of the year, rather than trying to perform all the necessary review work following the end of the period.

In the event that an auditor does not submit its report within this four-month period, it must write to the FCA to explain its failure to comply – including a full explanation of the reasons for its failure.

The FCA requires the firm to consider the auditor's draft report, and provide the auditor with information about any breach scenarios identified and any remedial actions implemented. The completed audit report should be shared with the firm's governing body as part of the evaluation of the effectiveness of the firm's systems to control the risks associated with client assets.

4.2   Content and Format of the Reasonable Assurance Engagement Report

A reasonable assurance engagement report will include the following elements:

Title	• Addressed to the FCA. • Statement that this is an independent reasonable assurance engagement report. • Name and FCA reference number of the firm.
Introduction	• Start and end dates of the period. • Confirmation that the report is prepared per SUP 3.10.4R. • Recognises that the FCA is the relevant regulator.
Basis of Opinion	• Statement that the auditor has met all of the procedures specified in the FRC standard. • Statement that the opinion relates only to the period under review. • Statement that the report gives no assurance to later periods.
Opinions	• Whether the firm maintained adequate systems to comply with specific CASS rules throughout the period. • Whether the firm was in compliance with those CASS rules as at the end of the period.

Opinion re Nominee involvement	• Where a subsidiary nominee formed part of the business model, an opinion as to whether adequate systems were maintained for the custody, identification, and control of custody assets held at the nominee (including reconciliations). *— acceptable nominee (records).*
Opinion re Client Money Distribution	• If a secondary pooling event took place during the period (such events will be discussed in chapter 8), whether the relevant rules were satisfied.
Breaches Schedule	• A statement confirming that the report must be read in conjunction with the Breaches Schedule attached (a record of all CASS-related breaches identified during the audit review or advised to the auditor by the firm).
Signature	• The audit firm is identified, noting the jurisdictions in which it operates. • The report is signed by the individual with primary responsibility within the audit firm. • The report is dated.

The Breaches Schedule must list each CASS breach identified within the period – whether identified by the firm or the auditor. For each breach the following must be recorded:

- a reference number for the breach (which may be a simple count within the Breach Schedule)
- rule reference(s) relevant to the breach
- the party which identified the breach   *why, who, what, comment.*
- details of the breach
- the firm's comments in response to the breach.

The auditor is responsible for the first four of these items, with the firm being required to provide its comments to the auditor so that the final column can be populated accordingly.

4.3   Content and Format of the Limited Assurance Engagement Report

The content of a limited assurance engagement report is broadly similar, though as such reports are applicable only where the firm advises that it held no client assets during the period, there are some important differences:

- The limited assurance engagement report will include an assertion from a director of the firm that no client assets were held during the period.
- The limited assurance engagement report will include no Breaches Schedule (as no CASS breaches should have arisen).
- The basis of the auditor's opinion is different, as the firm will not have performed all of the procedures specified by the FRC standard.
- Accordingly, the opinion statements are different.

A limited assurance engagement report will therefore include the following elements:

Title	• Addressed to the FCA. • Statement that this is an independent limited assurance engagement report. • Name and FCA reference number of the firm.
Introduction	• Start and end dates of the period. • Confirmation that the report is prepared per SUP 3.10.4R. • Recognises that the FCA is the relevant regulator.
Director Assertion/Regulatory Permission	• A statement confirming if the firm's permission does not allow it to hold client money and/or safe custody assets.
	• Confirmation that the directors of the firm have confirmed that the firm did not hold client money and/or safe custody assets during the period.
Basis of Opinion	• Statement that the auditor has met those procedures specified in the FRC standard that the auditor felt necessary to give limited assurance that no client assets were held. • Statement that the opinion relates only to the period under review. • Statement that the report gives no assurance to later periods.
Opinions	• Whether, based on the procedures reviewed, anything has come to the auditor's attention to indicate that client money and/or safe custody assets were held during the period.
Signature	• The audit firm is identified, noting the jurisdictions in which it operates. • The report is signed by the CASS engagement leader. • The report is dated.

[handwritten note in margin: essentially we can but we didn't.]

4.4 Audit Opinions: Qualified and Adverse

As shown in the tables above, an important part of either Assurance Engagement Report is the Auditor's opinion of the state of the firm's CASS controls. The FRC Client Asset Assurance Standard highlights two types of opinion that the auditor might make, according to the number and significance of weaknesses/ errors identified within the audit work performed.

A 'Qualified Opinion' is one in which the auditor concludes that the firm was generally in compliance with the CASS rules, though the auditor is of course obliged to qualify this assurance by listing the relevant breaches that had occurred during the period, ie, the firm is considered to be compliant aside from those breach items, and the written audit opinion statement will include language to the effect that '...except for...[the items identified]... the firm was compliant...'.

[handwritten note: Qualified by listing breaches]

More concerning for a firm would be if their CASS auditor was to give an 'Adverse Opinion'. An Adverse Opinion is one in which the auditor concludes that the firm's controls and activities fell short of the requirements of the CASS rules. Rather than simply experiencing some individual events that caused breaches, the firm's controls, systems, processes, or procedures were not sufficiently designed to achieve demonstrable compliance with CASS requirements. An Adverse Opinion will adopt language such as '...the firm did not maintain...' or '...the firm was not in compliance with...'.

more fundamentally problematic

On occasion an auditor may consider that it has not been able to see sufficient evidence to conclude its opinion, in which case it can record its inability to form an opinion – though must explain its reasons within the Client Assets Report in order that the FCA can understand the situation.

End of Chapter Questions

Think of an answer for each question and refer to the appropriate section for confirmation

1.   Rules in CASS 6 and CASS 7 require organisational arrangements to minimise the risk of
      diminution of client assets in respect of what four underlying causes?
      Answer reference: Section 1.1

2.   In respect of CASS 6 safe custody assets, what are the six types of event that would be notifiable
      to the FCA if they arose?
      Answer reference: Section 1.2

3.   For a CASS medium firm or CASS large firm, what are the three responsibilities of the person
      performing client asset operational oversight?
      Answer reference: Section 2

4.   What are the nine elements included in a client money and assets return (CMAR)?
      Answer reference: Section 2.3

5.   When is a client money and assets return (CMAR) required to be made?
      Answer reference: Section 2.3

6.   How is CASS oversight responsibility allocation achieved within a CASS small firm?
      Answer reference: Section 2.4

7.   What are the two types of CASS assurance engagement report that may be provided by the
      firm's auditor?
      Answer reference: Section 4.1

8.   Who must provide the CASS audit report to the Financial Conduct Authority (FCA), and what are
      the timescales for doing so?
      Answer reference: Section 4.1

9.   What is contained in the Breaches Schedule to a CASS audit report?
      Answer reference: Section 4.2

10.   A reasonable assurance engagement report will include three statements forming the basis of
      the auditor's opinion. What are these three statements?
      Answer reference: Section 4.2

11.   A reasonable assurance engagement must include the auditor's opinion on two matters, with
      two further opinions provided according to the firm's activity during the period. What are these
      four items of opinion?
      Answer reference: Section 4.2

Chapter Eight
When Problems Arise...

This syllabus area will provide approximately 5 of the 50 examination questions

8

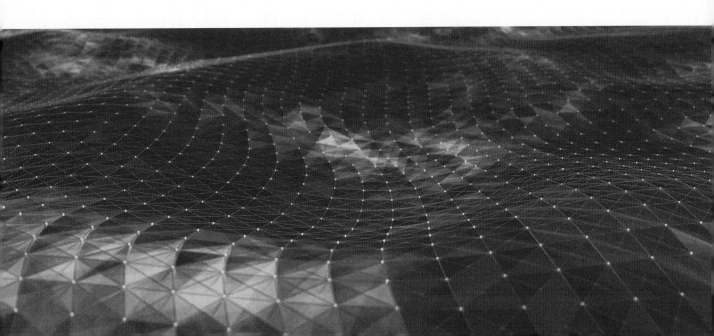

Introduction

We have explored what CASS requires of an investment firm, including certain types of event that would require the firm to notify the Financial Conduct Authority (FCA) of the problem encountered.

In this chapter, we will explore in more detail certain problems that can arise – some being problems that CASS helps the firm to manage, and others being the consequences for a firm if it fails to correctly understand and perform its obligations under the CASS rules.

We will also discuss how the Financial Services Compensation Scheme (FSCS) provides additional protection for investors.

1.   Financial Services Compensation Scheme (FSCS)

Learning Objective

8.1.1   Know in what circumstances the Financial Services Compensation Scheme will pay compensation, and how much

Investment involves taking financial risks in order to seek a profit, and potential losses must be accepted as a consequence. The purpose of the regulatory regime is to try and limit such potential losses to the core investments themselves, and prevent losses arising because a financial services firm through which the client is acting itself fails (becomes insolvent).

1.1   When Does the FSCS Provide Compensation?

The FSCS becomes active when a financial services firm goes into 'default', ie, when it fails to pay its obligations to customers under the regulatory regime. The FSCS will cover losses that arise on deposits, investment business, home finance, insurance policies, and insurance broking. If any customer of a financial services firm considers that the company has defaulted, resulting in a loss from one of these areas, the customer can claim against the FSCS.

1.2   How Much Compensation is Available?

The FSCS is financially supported by the industry, through a levy paid by regulated firms. The amount of cover available from the scheme is therefore limited, with the level set for different types of product reflecting a typical investor's exposure.

The following table summarises the current amounts of compensation available for a valid claim in respect of the business covered by this workbook:

Type of Activity	Protection Available
Deposits	100% of the deposit value, up to a maximum of £85,000 per person per banking licence. In addition, there is a £1 million protection limit for temporary high balances held by a bank, building society, or credit union.
Investments	100% of the value of the investments lost, up to a maximum of £85,000 per person per firm. (Remember: the compensation relates to the firm being unable to deliver assets that should have been held for the client, or failing to provide any investment return that was specifically guaranteed. Normal investment losses are not protected by the FSCS).

The COMP Sourcebook includes more information regarding the FSCS claims process, such as identifying eligible claimants, and other qualifying conditions for a claim.

2. Client Money Distribution and Transfer (CASS 7A)

Learning Objective

8.2.1 Know the definitions of a primary pooling event and a secondary pooling event

8.2.2 Know how client money is treated in a primary pooling event

8.2.3 Know how client money is treated in a secondary pooling event

All of the controls discussed within this workbook are intended to ensure that, in the event of a firm's default, it should be possible to return to each client the correct value of assets and money held by the firm on their behalf. In CASS, such a return of client money is referred to as a 'client money distribution'.

CASS uses the word 'pool' to describe a given aggregate sum of money (for example, the amount of money held within a particular client bank account (CBA)) held for a specific group of clients. In many cases, a firm will operate one general pool of client money, with the money of all clients mixed together, so that each client has a claim on money held in any of the CBAs operated in the firm's name. However, we noted in chapter 3 that designated CBAs or designated client fund accounts would produce additional 'pools' if the bank concerned was to fail (in contrast to the firm itself failing).

As we now approach the scenario where some failure has occurred, we will find that understanding the 'pools' of client money that exist becomes increasingly important to resolving the position. CASS defines two types of client money distribution, depending on the legal entity that has failed:

- **primary pooling event (PPE)**, and
- **secondary pooling event (SPE).**

Pooling events

2.1 What Events Trigger a Primary Pooling Event (PPE)?

Four different types of event will trigger a PPE under CASS 7A:

1. Failure of the firm (ie, the legal entity holding client money on behalf of the client becomes insolvent). *or the hive*

2. Vesting of assets in a trustee in accordance with an 'assets requirement' imposed under the Financial Services and Markets Act (FSMA).

3. Imposition in the firm's FCA permission of a requirement relating to all client money held by the firm. *FCA says you have to.*

4. Where a firm is unable to correctly identify and allocate in its records any valid claims arising as a result of a secondary pooling event (SPE) (which will be explained later in section 2.3). CASS does confirm that this last trigger of a PPE applies only if the firm has no reasonable grounds to expect that it can rectify the position in a reasonable period.

Q

For simplicity, the following discussion will assume that the first of these four trigger events has arisen: that a firm holding client money for its client has become insolvent.

2.2 What is the Consequence of a Primary Pooling Event (PPE)?

The key consequence of the PPE is that all client money pools that existed prior to the firm becoming insolvent must be effectively frozen. Any new money that is received by the firm after the insolvency event must either be immediately returned to the sender or, if kept by the firm, be placed into a CBA that is fully separate from any CBA already in use for that pre-liquidation pool. *either returned to client or held separate*

This causes fundamental operational problems if the firm is engaged in high-volume retail investment business, as it is likely that investment instructions and payments will continue to arrive in the post even though the firm is now under insolvency law, with an insolvency practitioner assessing the best course of action (for example: close the firm, or sell the firm to a new owner who will honour any debts in place). *Prior business still operates w/t CBA*

CASS notes that any money received after the PPE which relates to investment business contracted prior to the PPE should continue to be accepted by the firm within the pre-PPE client money pool. This is a sensible position, as the FCA wants to see stable markets; as such, it is best if any market commitments entered into by the firm prior to its insolvency are able to settle – to avoid contagion to other firms if market commitments are voided. In order to settle those transactions, the firm is likely to require the use of any money owed by the client concerned, and so CASS 7A expects the firm to continue to receive such monies and allocate them within the original relevant client money pool.

using client money to settle prior transactions.

While this approach is therefore sensible in terms of maintaining market stability, it again increases the operational complexity for a firm undergoing a PPE – in respect of any sum of money received after the PPE, the firm must decide into which of at least two client money pools that money should be applied.

every bit of money you ettes into a before or afk

In theory, providing this separation between pools is achieved, within approximately one week all market transactions should have settled and the client money (and associated safe custody assets) should be reconciled and be ready to be released to the individual clients concerned. Some of the standard CASS controls described earlier are suspended in respect of a client money pool that is undergoing a PPE.

If the insolvency practitioner concludes that the firm can continue in operation, then any such ongoing business should be conducted in the separate post-PPE client money pool. Standard CASS controls would continue in effect for that continuing business. *i) then stay, unrelevon .*

It is hoped that the PPE process (while having much potential operational complexity) will enable clients to receive their money swiftly, reduce the likelihood of contagion following failure of a firm, and enable an insolvency practitioner to consider continuing the firm's business activity while sorting out the original failure event.

2.3 What Events Trigger a Secondary Pooling Event (SPE)?

A secondary pooling event occurs if a third party fails while holding client money on behalf of a firm (eg, if a bank holding client money becomes insolvent).

Consider the following example of a firm operating a single client money pool, currently containing a total of £5,000 of client money with its bank ('First Standard Bank'):

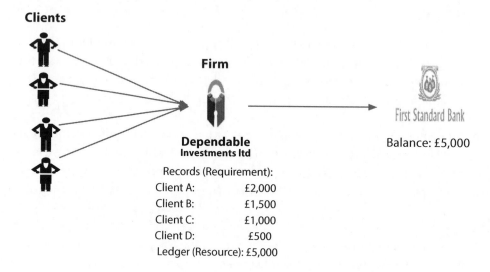

We can see the firm's internal ledger position, which shows a balanced position for resource and requirement (assuming there are no outstanding settlements, prudent segregation or unallocated sums, for example). We can also see the balance recorded by First Standard Bank, and see that the external client money reconciliation is also balanced.

Suppose that First Standard Bank announces that it can no longer honour sums deposited with it. Dependable can no longer consider that the £5,000 is available to it, so must write down its bank ledger accordingly:

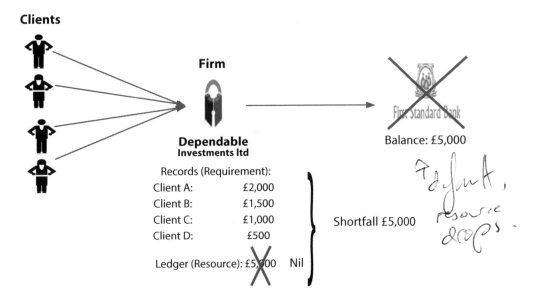

At this point Dependable has a choice. It might use its corporate cash to resolve the shortfall (in the same way as it would resolve any other shortfall identified as part of the reconciliation cycle), and if the shortfall amount is relatively small this might well be the preferred course of action. By opening/activating a client bank account held at a different bank (say 'Southern State Bank'), and depositing at that second bank sufficient cash to clear the shortfall arising at First Standard Bank, the firm can resolve the secondary pooling event and return to a balanced position:

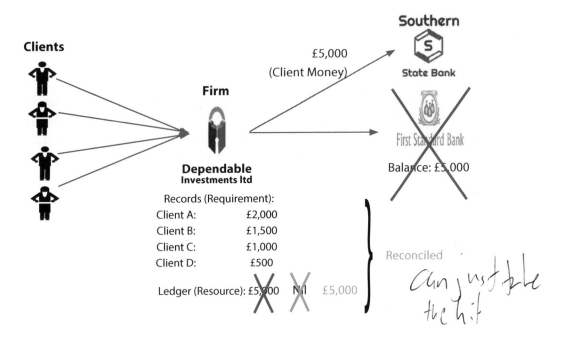

While CASS 7A therefore provides a theoretical approach to resolving the problems of a bank becoming insolvent, it should be noted that in reality there may be a considerable delay in opening a fresh CBA with an alternative bank. Some firms may already operate CBAs with multiple banks, which could potentially be of benefit were one of those banks to fail, though such an approach would only be successful if those accounts formed part of the same pre-event client money pool.

2.4   What is the Consequence of a Secondary Pooling Event (SPE)?

If the firm is unable to resolve the SPE in the manner outlined above (by placing a corresponding balance of corporate money into a different CBA that can be applied to the same client money pool as that experiencing the SPE), the firm is obliged to take different action to resolve the shortfall arising.

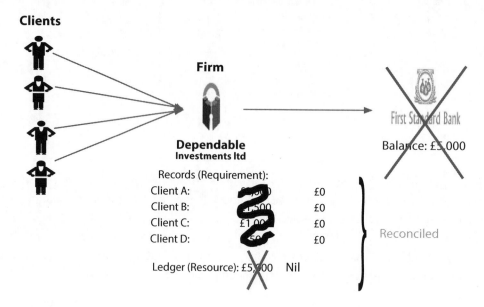

While it may be surprising (given the effort that each regulated firm must expend each day in order to ensure that client money balances are known, recorded, and reconciled), if the firm cannot resolve the SPE by making up the shortfall into a different CBA, CASS 7A requires the firm to instead write down the client entitlements to client money in line with the shortfall that has arisen. In the example here, the full balance of client money is considered lost, and so all client balances must be written down by 100% to zero. In the event that only some of the client money balance has been lost, each client in the affected client money pool would see their balance reduced pro rata to the overall balance.

The firm will then continue to perform its standard CASS controls each day as usual – but using the written-down figures for its client ledger and requirement values.

The firm may still expect that in the future it can recover the lost money – either because the bank's insolvency practitioner will return money previously held in the CBA (in whole or in part), or by way of a claim against the FSCS on behalf of the affected investors. As such, CASS 7A requires the firm to make a record of the amounts by which each investor's balance has been written down.

temporarily take out of client balances –

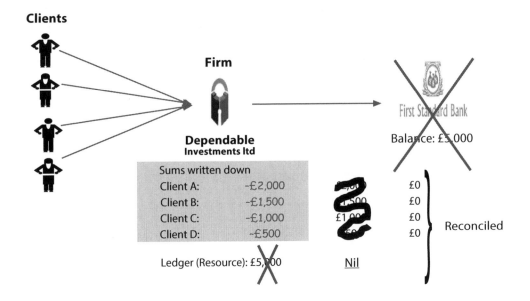

If the firm recovers any money relating to the client money pool which incurred the SPE, such money must be re-credited to the affected clients, pro rata against the firm's record of the sums by which their client entitlement was reduced.

It is therefore hoped that this process could result in all clients receiving back some money due to them, but without the bank failure also pushing the firm into insolvency. However, as noted above, if a firm finds that it has lost control of the records being used to manage an SPE, that fact alone can require the firm to enter a PPE (without the firm itself being insolvent). *— not knowing how much each client is owed can mean a PPE.*

3.   CASS Resolution Pack (CASS 10)

Learning Objective

8.3.1   Understand the purpose of a CASS resolution pack

8.3.2   Know the contents of and the requirements for updating a CASS resolution pack

8.3.3   Understand the timeframes for retrieval of this information and what this means for operational support

8.3.4   Know the firms' obligations to notify the FCA of breaches in accordance with CASS 10

As we have seen, insolvency of a firm is a critical time for ensuring that client assets are properly protected – particularly as an insolvency practitioner will usually be appointed to oversee the management of the failed company. Such an insolvency practitioner is likely to have some familiarity with financial services businesses, but will not have a pre-existing understanding of how this particular firm may operate, or how to navigate the firm's records and data archives to best effect.

For this reason, the FCA requires that all firms holding client money and/or safe custody assets must maintain a **CASS Resolution Pack** (CASS RP) – effectively a guide to an incoming insolvency practitioner containing certain key information that will be required to enable the business to be correctly managed, and confirming how other important data can be retrieved.

CASS guidebook on how to wind up company

3.1   What Does a CASS Resolution Pack Contain?

The CASS RP contains two broad types of material:

- summary information about how the firm operates (including matters like the banks at which client money is held), and   *Summary of firm.*
- certain 'business-as-usual' materials that should be retrieved for inclusion in the CASS RP in the event of the firm's failure.   *– what BAU material to get.*

Some materials must be available immediately, while others can be provided within 48 hours of the insolvency occurring. Note that the firm should therefore ensure it has made arrangements for the retrieval of this material even if the firm's staff are no longer available to fulfil such a request. This may include paying a retainer to an outsourcing service provider to extract data for the CASS RP and provide it to an insolvency practitioner even if the firm may no longer exist to pay its outstanding fees.

– Someone has to be able to get it up.

CASS 10 sets out the requirements for the CASS RP. The following list of documentation must be assembled specifically to be part of the CASS RP in the event of the firm's failure:

where's first stuff

- A master document containing the information needed to retrieve each of the underlying materials making up the CASS RP (such information might include file locations in the firm's network drives, or the report names etc. that would be required to obtain the material from a third party).
- A document confirming each institution used by the firm to hold client money or client safe custody assets.   *– who holds stuff. and what agreements you have*
- A copy of the executed agreements, including side letters and acknowledgement letters, entered into with each of the institutions holding client money or client safe custody assets.
- A document identifying each appointed representative, tied agent, field agent, or other agent receiving client money or safe custody assets in its capacity as agent of the firm.   *agent CM,*
- A document confirming each senior manager and director (or equivalent) within the firm who is critical or important to the performance of operational functions relating to CASS. The nature of their responsibility should be recorded. This list should include the individual having CASS operational oversight responsibility.   *who is important? why*
- Documentation identifying any related group company involved in any CASS obligations of the firm (eg, a group company acting as nominee).
- Documentation confirming any third party performing operational functions relating to CASS 6 or CASS 7 on behalf of the firm (ie, any outsourced service providers).
- A copy of the executed agreements, including, for example, side letters, entered into with each outsourced service provider.
- Where the firm relies on a third party for CASS processing, a document confirming how to gain access to the relevant information held by that third party and effect a transfer of any client money or safe custody assets held by the firm but controlled by that third party.
- A copy of the firm's procedures manual relating to the management, recording and transfer of client money/safe custody assets that it holds (ie, procedures for CASS-related processes that the incoming insolvency practitioner would need to perform).

any third parties –   to procedures

The context of outsourcing must be considered, as many firms use outsourced service providers and the items listed above include some that specifically relate to outsourced services. The fundamental purpose of the CASS RP is to enable the incoming insolvency practitioner to efficiently understand how the firm has structured its CASS activities, in order to operationally replace the failed firm. The procedures required are therefore the procedures of the firm (and not the procedures of any outsourced service provider) – and the firm must specifically confirm in its CASS RP what activities had been outsourced prior to the insolvency, together with details of how the insolvency practitioner can gain access to data held by a third party and affect a transfer of any assets held by a third party. (Remember that using a third party to hold assets on behalf of the firm is not a form of 'outsourcing'. The list above distinguishes between (a) institutions holding client assets for the firm, and (b) third parties performing operational functions of the firm).

The internal operational procedures of an outsourced service provider are not required by the CASS RP; the focus is the procedures of the firm (as the insolvency practitioner will need to follow those procedures in order to exercise control over the assets). In many cases, the firm's contract with the outsourced service provider may terminate if the firm becomes insolvent, and so the firm should ensure that any such termination does not expose the assets to risk (hence the importance of contracts and side letters being included in the CASS RP). Such information enables the incoming insolvency practitioner to consider – in light of whether the business will be a running concern – whether any outsourced services are required or whether the outsourcing arrangements can simply be allowed to terminate.

Note that the regulatory requirement is to retrieve the most recent version of the CASS RP materials completed prior to the firm becoming insolvent. CASS 10 specifically states that these items should not be generated following the insolvency of the firm. Consequently, any material changes to documents in the CASS RP are required to be included in documentation within five business days of the changes. Staff in the affected areas need to be made aware of this and controls need to be put into place to ensure that this deadline has been met and that all documents are therefore up to date. The following list summarises the existing 'business-as-usual' documentation that must be retrieved in order to complete the CASS RP:

- selection/appropriateness of a third party holding safe custody assets
- details of consent by clients who have permitted the firm to use their safe custody assets
- records confirming each client's entitlement to specific safe custody assets and client money held
- executed client agreements including any right to use safe custody assets
- the most recent safe custody asset reconciliations and controls, including the date performed, the actions taken to perform the control, any discrepancies identified, and the actions taken to resolve those discrepancies
- the most recent internal and external client money reconciliations, including the date performed, the actions taken to perform the reconciliation, and the outcome of the calculation of client money resource vs client money requirement
- policies and procedures for the carrying out of record checks and reconciliations
- records confirming the grounds on which the firm considered each third party to be appropriate to hold client money
- the categorisation of each client (as retail, professional or eligible counterparty), plus any notice issued to the client to confirm their categorisation
- copies of all client agreements entered into.

3.2   Additional FCA Requirements Relating to the CASS RP

An incomplete or outdated CASS RP would therefore risk causing confusion in the event of a firm's insolvency; the insolvency practitioner might not be able to locate all the assets held for the firm, or might waste time trying to investigate old reconciliation differences that the firm had in fact already resolved. However, maintaining an accurate and current CASS RP requires time and effort by the firm (given the amount of documentation involved).

The CASS 10 rules, therefore, confirm that the firm should be able to extract the required records within 48 hours of an insolvency practitioner (or similar individual) being appointed over the firm's affairs. While this is a rare and unlikely event, which could result in firms not wrestling with the practical reality of this deadline, firms should be aware that the rules also enable the FCA to request any firm to provide it with a complete CASS RP within the same 48-hour period. The FCA, therefore, has the ability to actively test any firm's readiness to generate a CASS RP – and the firm's CASS auditor may also ask about the firm's readiness to do so.

Again, in recognition of the importance of the CASS RP in the event of a firm's insolvency, the FCA has also included a notifiable breach requirement relating to the CASS RP. If the firm has not maintained its CASS RP, or has been unable to extract the material in line with the CASS 10 rules, that fact is a notifiable breach that must be reported in writing immediately to the FCA.

4.   Consequences of Regulatory Failure

Learning Objective

8.4.1   Know the historical background, including key cases that have shaped the regime

We must consider one last form of failure: the failure of a firm to operate in line with the requirements of CASS. If the firm fails to establish an operational environment that satisfies CASS, the firm will be exposed to the risk of regulatory sanction by the FCA. FCA action could begin as a result of the auditor issuing an adverse or qualified CASS audit report, or following the firm notifying the FCA that its key CASS controls are not being effected as required. Regulatory investigation is time-consuming for a firm to manage, so even if the firm successfully defends itself and is not subject to a financial penalty, there will still be a financial cost in its defence activity.

This is another example of why it is important that a firm can clearly, concisely, and comprehensively explain to a third party (in this case, the FCA) how its organisational arrangements for CASS function, and demonstrate that the overall approach is robust.

4.1   Past Regulatory Action

The FCA publishes details of all regulatory sanctions it issues. Such 'final notices' provide details of the failures observed in the firm, how those failures were identified, whether such warning signals were heeded or ignored, and the period of time for which the failures were allowed to exist. In the case of CASS events, the final notice will usually indicate the value of client assets that were exposed to potential loss as a result of the failures concerned.

There have been over a dozen CASS-related financial sanctions issued by the FCA, ranging from relatively small sums (£12,000) up to substantial sums (the current record being a penalty of £126 million).

Often the final notice will record that the firm failed to satisfy various FCA Principles – often Principle 3 and Principle 10 – because the mechanisms to protect client money and/or safe custody assets were flawed or incomplete in some way.

Some of the most significant failings identified in past regulatory action include the failure to:

- properly segregate client assets from corporate assets
- perform appropriate compliance reviews of the CASS processes
- perform client money calculations of resource vs requirement
- notify the FCA of relevant CASS 6 and CASS 7 failures
- monitor and manage the firm's appointed representatives
- segregate the correct sum relating to margined products
- obtain/maintain acknowledgement letters for CBAs
- establish the necessary controls over client money held in money market deposits
- sufficiently identify the legal entity to which internal records belonged (as noted below).

The largest fine yet issued by the FCA related to a pair of group companies that together failed to record the correct legal entity on asset records, a situation that had continued for almost six years. As a result, the FCA concluded that the asset reconciliations were incorrect, which also made the CASS RP and client money and assets return (CMAR) reporting of the firm inaccurate over that full period. The FCA also found that client assets had been mixed with corporate assets, and that the firm had settled client transactions using assets of other clients.

While there can be little defence for a firm that has failed to correctly interpret and apply the CASS rules to its business, it should be noted that the firms in question were all subject to an annual CASS audit. A final notice issued in December 2020 demonstrated this point. The FCA's comments indicate that the firm had misunderstood its relationship with a group company located in the US; some individuals thought the firm had outsourced work to the US, while other individuals believed that the UK firm had effectively introduced business to the US company (without itself having responsibility for the client's assets). As a result of incorrectly understanding its own business model, the UK firm performed regulated activity for which it had not gained FCA authorisation. Having not understood that its business model included responsibility for client assets, the firm failed to establish the processes and controls needed to comply with the CASS rules, and it was the CASS Auditor who identified that client assets were in fact held by the firm. The FCA's investigation highlighted a catalogue of failings and non-existent controls, which resulted in the firm being fined £8.96m.

The FCA's level of concern at CASS compliance, combined with the value of fines being applied for CASS failures, has increased the sensitivity of auditors to any CASS failings identified. While it is important that auditors apply consistent standards when performing their audit engagement work, it is also important that they exercise their professional skills to assess the arrangements that each firm has put in place, in light of the specific decisions that firm has taken in respect of client money and safe custody assets, rather than expecting to see all firms apply a single approach to CASS compliance. The audit relationship must be able to support robust discussions between firm and auditor, to ensure correct understanding of the processes and any weaknesses identified by the auditor in the operation of those processes.

End of Chapter Questions

Think of an answer for each question and refer to the appropriate section for confirmation

1. What is the Financial Services Compensation Scheme (FSCS)?
    Answer reference: Section 1.1 *[handwritten] Deposit or investment loss for retail firms,*

2. The Financial Services Compensation Scheme (FSCS) protects investors up to certain value limits. What limit applies to losses from deposit activity? *[handwritten] 85k. PP per firm.*
    Answer reference: Section 1.2

3. When an investment falls in value, resulting in loss for the investor, what level of protection is available from the Financial Services Compensation Scheme (FSCS)? *[handwritten] O*
    Answer reference: Section 1.2

4. What four types of event can trigger a primary pooling event (PPE)?
    Answer reference: Section 2.1 *[handwritten] ① failure of firm   ?* *[handwritten] ②*

5. What is a secondary pooling event (SPE)?
    Answer reference: Section 2.3 *[handwritten] when bank fails*

6. When a secondary pooling event (SPE) occurs, the firm must choose between two courses of action. One action is to use corporate money to immediately resolve the resulting shortfall via a separate client bank account. What is the other option available to the firm?
    Answer reference: Section 2.4 *[handwritten] Writedown Client money*

7. What is the purpose of a CASS resolution pack (CASS RP)?
    Answer reference: Section 3 *[handwritten] Swift resolution/return of ? sub's*

8. What 'business-as-usual' documents must be collated when completing a CASS resolution pack (CASS RP)? *[handwritten] All*
    Answer reference: Section 3.1

9. What contracts need to be included in the firm's CASS resolution pack (CASS RP)?
    Answer reference: Section 3.1 *[handwritten] w/ all third parties*

10. In what ways would a regulatory investigation impact a firm?
    Answer reference: Section 4 *[handwritten] £ .*

[handwritten] il 1e

Chapter Nine
The Client

This syllabus area will provide approximately 4 of the 50 examination questions

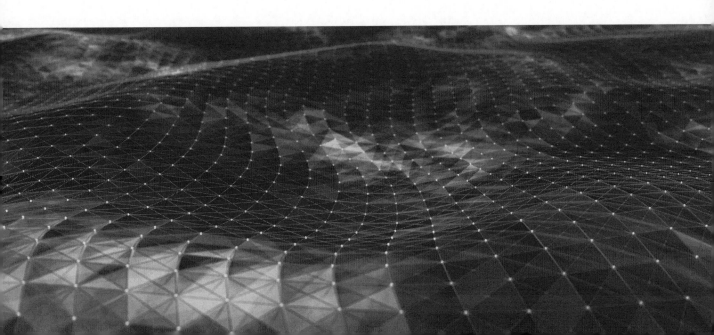

Introduction

In chapter 1, we considered the basics of legal contracts between the parties, and the contracts entered into effect investment activity, we can now revisit these arrangements in light of all the detail we have considered.

We have now seen that the full relationships needed to support investment transactions would be illustrated as follows:

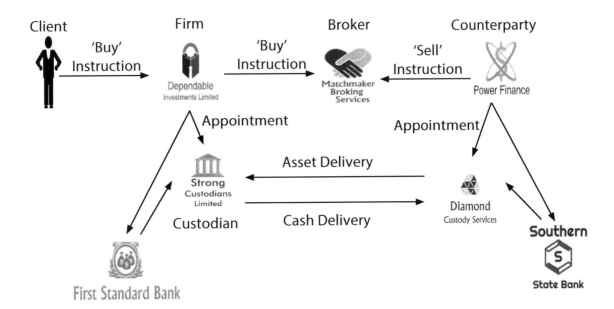

Instructions move between the regulated firms to match a trade in the market. Both Dependable Investments ltd ('Dependable') and 'Power Finance' each need to instruct their custodians to deliver or receive assets, and instruct any cash movements necessary between their respective banks and custodians, so that the various contractual settlement obligations can be effected on settlement date.

Given the potential that a mistake anywhere in this network could result in a failed settlement, it is important that Dependable knows exactly what its obligations are to its client – and these will be set out in its client agreement (sometimes known as 'terms and conditions' or 'terms of business').

We will also look in this chapter at certain obligations that the firm has under CASS in respect of reporting to its clients, and ensuring that information held by the firm (such as the client's bank account details) are not misused. We will additionally note how the categorisation of a client as a professional customer can reduce the burden of CASS compliance for the firm.

1. Client Types and CASS Exemptions

Learning Objective

9.1.1   Know the application of the client money rules to: professional clients (and the professional client opt-out); affiliates; credit institutions and approved banks

We have noted some of these considerations in earlier chapters; however, we can summarise the points here.

1.1   Professional Clients

The FCA rules distinguish between retail clients and professional clients – based on criteria such as whether the client is itself regulated, has experience of market investing, or has investable assets exceeding a certain value. A professional client is therefore assumed to have superior knowledge and understanding of the financial services market. Accordingly, we have seen that CASS rules will allow a firm to perform certain types of activity for a professional client that would not be permitted for a retail client (eg, title transfer collateral arrangements (TTCAs)).

In most cases, the CASS rules apply equally when the firm is contracting with a professional client as with a retail client. However, the following differences are worth noting:

- If the firm is enabling the client to invest in a non-UK market in which assets can only be registered in the name of the firm (rather than the client, a nominee, or a third party), prior written consent is required if dealing for a retail client, while the firm need only notify a professional client of the approach being taken.
- For non-MiFID business only, the 'professional client opt-out' enables a firm to allow a professional client to choose whether their money should be handled as client money or not. While it may seem unlikely that a client would voluntarily allow the firm to not apply the various protections set out in CASS, it should be noted that foregoing certain protections might be necessary in order that the firm can access certain assets or certain markets on behalf of the client. A professional client is deemed to have sufficient understanding to make such a decision in respect of their investment activity.
- The *de minimis* level for paying allocated but unclaimed client money away to charity is higher for a professional client (£100) than for a retail client (£25).

1.2   Affiliates

It is possible that one of a firm's clients might be an affiliated company of the firm. Generally, such a position does not affect the CASS controls and protections afforded to that client's assets.

However, there are some cases where the nature of the relationship does affect the application of the CASS rules:

- Where a firm is safeguarding and administering investments in respect of the non-MiFID business of an affiliated company, the custody rules (CASS 6) do not apply unless either of the following two criteria apply.

- the affiliated company is being treated as an 'arm's length' client (ie, treated as any other client of the firm), or
- the firm has been notified that the designated investments concerned belong to one or more clients of the affiliated company.
- Where the firm holds or receives client money in respect of the non-MiFID business of an affiliated company, the client money rules (CASS 7) do not apply unless any of the following three criteria apply:
  - the affiliated company is being treated as an 'arm's length' client (ie, treated as any other client of the firm)
  - the firm has been notified that the money concerned belongs to one or more clients of the affiliated company, or
  - the affiliated company is either the manager of an occupational pension scheme or is an overseas company and has notified the firm that the money is to be treated as client money as it relates to the affiliated company's work for its own clients.

1.3   Credit Institutions and Approved Banks

We have already noted that the so-called 'banking exemption' applies to firms that are authorised to accept deposits and have confirmed to their clients that any monies received are being handled as deposits rather than sums of client money. CASS 7 does not therefore apply where the credit institution or approved bank treats the money as a deposit.

1.4   Trustees/Depositaries of UCITS funds and Alternative Investment Funds (AIFs)

While not an 'exemption' as such, it should be noted that the CASS rules has very specific application to firms that are acting as trustee/depositary of collective funds (whether UCITS funds or AIFs). Affected firms will need to assess the detailed requirements within CASS to determine the individual rules that are applicable to their business model, but in general the key points to note are:

- The trustee/depositary of a UCITS/AIF are not subject to CASS 7 rules for client money.
- The trustee/depositary of a UCITS/AIF is generally subject to other chapters of CASS (including, for example, the CASS 6 rules relating to the assets held by the depositary on behalf of the fund).
- When applying CASS rules to its business, the trustee/depositary of a UCITS/AIF should interpret 'client' to mean the fund to which it acts as trustee/depositary.

2. Mandates (CASS 8)

Learning Objective

9.2.1 Know the definition of a mandate

9.2.2 Understand the circumstances that may give rise to a mandate

9.2.3 Know what records and internal controls have to be maintained in respect of mandates

---

The mandate rules in CASS 8 are very different from the CASS 6 and CASS 7 obligations we have considered so far. The CASS 8 rules are intended to reduce the risk to clients where the client provides the firm with information that would enable the firm to exercise control over assets of the client held outside of the firm's domain. However, application of these rules within a firm can become complicated as the rules address what the firm would be capable of doing with the information, rather than what it is permitted or authorised by the client to do with that information.

It should also be noted that the word 'mandate' is commonly used by various firms to denote an authority or instruction held. The CASS use of the language is therefore very different to the usual way the term is used within a regulated firm, and care should be taken when discussing CASS 8 Mandates to ensure that the scope of the discussion is correctly drawn.

2.1 Definition of a CASS Mandate

CASS defines a 'mandate' as being 'any means' that would enable the firm to control a client's assets (or liabilities) – providing that five specific conditions are satisfied. For example, if a firm receives its customers debit card details or bank account details (both of which would enable the firm to send instructions to collect the client's money) those would be 'means' in the context of CASS 8. If those 'means' satisfied the five conditions then those 'means' would also be a CASS 8 Mandate.

[handwritten: mandate = control of client's money not under management]

The five conditions are as follows (with some comments added to illustrate the subtle implications of each):

1. The 'means' must be obtained by the firm from the client and with the client's consent, ie, if the firm obtains the necessary information by some other source, then according to the rules such information would not constitute a CASS 8 Mandate. *[handwritten: from the client directly]*
2. If the 'means' is obtained in respect of insurance mediation activity, the information must be received in written form, ie, if a firm receives the client's debit card details during a telephone call in order to pay an insurance premium, there is no CASS 8 Mandate created. *[handwritten: written]*
3. The 'means' must be retained by the firm. This is a complex matter, and so CASS 8 gives additional information on the retention of data. In essence, CASS 8 recognises that in order to use the data even one time, the firm will usually need to make a record of it. However, if the firm does not subsequently delete that record, the data is considered to have been 'retained' even if the firm has no intention to submit further collections using that information, ie, the fact that the 'means' has been 'retained' in the firm's records would satisfy this condition, regardless of whether the firm intends to make subsequent use of that 'means'.

4. The 'means' would enable the firm to instruct another party (such as the client's bank) without any additional involvement of the client being required. Note that this relates to capability to create an instruction, rather than the client having authorised each such instruction, ie, if the firm has the client's bank account details and could submit an electronic direct debit instruction, which would be honoured by the client's bank without being pre-approved on each occasion by the client concerned, that would satisfy this condition.

5. The 'means' enables the firm to give one of the following types of instruction:

   a. instruction to another person (such as a bank) to affect money held by that person for the client

   b. instruction to another person (such as a financial services firm) to affect a client entitlement maintained by that person for the client (including money held under either CASS 5 or CASS 7)

   c. instruction to another person (such as a custodian) to affect a safe custody asset of the client held by that person, or

   d. instruction to another person such that the client would incur a debt to that person (or some other person) as a result.

In simple terms: if the firm receives from its client and retains the information necessary to instruct an external party and as a result affect the money or assets of the client held other than by the firm, the firm holds a CASS 8 Mandate. The following list includes example scenarios in which a CASS 8 Mandate would exist:

- A client wants to set up a direct debit so that the firm can collect money from a different bank account of the client. The client provides their bank details (whether in writing or via other channels), which the firm retains (in paper or electronic form) and uses to instruct the cash collections from the bank concerned.

- A client authorises the firm to be able to instruct transactions against an account of the client held at a separate custodian. The firm stores the account information for future use, and understands that any such instructions will simply be accepted by the external custodian without the client being asked to re-confirm each separate transaction.

- A client provides their debit card/credit card details so that the firm can collect money each time periodic fees are due. If the firm directly receives and stores the card details then a CASS 8 Mandate exists. (However, it should be noted that in respect of e-commerce it is becoming common for a firm to use an independent party to effect the actual cash collections without the firm's own IT systems ever receiving or storing the actual card details – and where the firm does not retain the card details there is no CASS 8 Mandate.)

2.2   Controls Relating to CASS Mandates

Given that CASS 8 considers a mandate to be any 'means' that enables the firm to instruct movement of the client's assets held by another party, the key control required by CASS 8 is to maintain a list of all mandates obtained by the firm.

This list must include details of any conditions that the client or the firm has placed on the use of the mandate (remember that the 'means' remains a mandate even if the firm has no expectation of making future use of the information). As such, a 'condition' might include the amounts to be collected, or the frequency of collections – so might include the resumption date of a direct debit collection following an agreed payment holiday.

This list must be retained in a manner that enables it to be provided to an auditor completing the CASS audit, and may be requested by the FCA. The CASS rules also include certain pieces of information that must be included in the list of mandates where the 'means' was received in non-written form (such as via a telephone call). The following five points are quoted directly from CASS 8:

1. the nature of the mandate (eg, debit card details)
2. the purpose of the mandate (eg, collecting insurance premiums)
3. how the mandate was obtained (eg, by telephone)
4. the name of the relevant client, and
5. the date on which the mandate was obtained.

[handwritten margin notes: details what; Reason why; how; who; when]

In addition to the list of mandates, the firm should also maintain the following controls:

[handwritten margin note: trans; check that trans are done as per instructions give]

- a record of each transaction entered into under each mandate held
- internal controls to ensure that each transaction entered into under each mandate is carried out in line with any conditions placed on the mandate by either the client or the firm's management
- a summary of procedures and internal controls for giving instructions under the mandates held by the firm, and
- where the firm holds a passbook or similar documentation of the client, internal controls for protecting such material.

[handwritten margin note: audit history]

Once a firm destroys its record of the 'means', it ceases to hold a CASS 8 Mandate. However, it should continue to ensure that it can demonstrate that the mandate had been subject to the correct controls (for a period of at least one year, or at least five years if the mandate related to MiFID business). An audit trail of any changes to the list of mandates must be retained, so that it is clear what has changed and on what date any changes have been made.

The above mechanisms seem based upon the perception that a given firm's approach to securing such information will be highly segregated. In an IT-based industry however, the client records are likely to be highly integrated – such that creating a 'list of mandates' may well require the firm to create a report that serves no distinct operational purpose aside from demonstrating compliance with CASS 8. These particular CASS rules therefore create additional record-keeping requirements for many firms, and the specific data to be included can be a source of tension for some firms.

3. Client Reporting (CASS 9)

Learning Objective

9.3.1   Know the obligations regarding reporting to clients contained in CASS 9

3.1   General Reporting to Clients

The firm's obligations on reporting to its clients are largely found in the Conduct of Business Sourcebook (COBS) Sourcebook. CASS 9 notes the COBS obligation to provide information about the firm's custody arrangements when commencing business for a new client.

CASS 9 also reminds firms of the COBS requirement to provide each client with an annual periodic statement of client money and safe custody assets held. The minimum frequency for providing these statements is quarterly for MiFID business, and annually in other cases. However, CASS 9 adds two specific expectations in respect of this report.

Firstly, it obliges the firm to issue upon request from the client a duplicate of a report previously provided. Such requests should be satisfied within five business days of receipt.

Secondly, CASS 9 obliges the firm to provide an ad hoc statement upon request from the client, showing the current client money and assets held.

In both cases, CASS 9 allows the firm to receive a fee for the additional effort – providing that fee reasonably corresponds to the costs incurred by the firm. (Note: there is no equivalent ability to recover costs for issuing the original annual statement of client money and safe custody assets held.)

CASS 9 also highlights that any statement should clarify which of the money or assets listed are held subject to the respective CASS 6 and CASS 7 rules and which are not.

CASS 9 also reminds firms of their COBS obligations to provide factual information to each client about the ways that safe custody assets and client money will be held on their behalf.

3.2   Prime Brokerage Services

CASS 9 also includes obligations for a firm providing prime brokerage services to provide a daily statement of the client assets held in relation to those services. These statements must reflect the values and positions as at close of business on the statement date, and be provided by close of business on the following business day.

The statement must include the following:

- The total value of client money and safe custody assets held by the firm for that client.
- The location of all safe custody assets (including those held with a subcustodian).
- A list of all institutions holding client money (whether in client bank accounts (CBAs) or client transaction accounts (CTAs)).

- The total collateral held by the firm in respect of secured prime brokerage transactions
- The cash values of each of the following:
  - cash loans made to the client (including accrued interest)
  - securities to be redelivered by that client in respect of open short positions
  - short sale cash proceeds held by the firm
  - the current settlement amount arising under futures contracts
  - cash margin held by the firm in respect of open futures contracts
  - mark-to-market close-out exposure of any 'over-the-counter' transactions secured using safe custody assets or client money
  - all other safe custody assets held by the firm for that client.

4. Client Relationships, Contracts and Agreements

Learning Objective

9.4.1 Understand the purpose of client agreements

9.4.2 Know the different types of agreement depending on the service provided, and the main clauses that impact on the administration of the client account

We can now apply all that we have learned about the decisions a firm will take in determining its business model, and consider the firm-client relationship in greater detail than in chapter 1.

The client relationship is central to everything that a regulated firm does – not only in respect of CASS. The firm must know the identity of its clients to ensure that it protects against money laundering. The relationship must clearly be created between a specific regulated firm and the client (whether an individual or some corporate entity that has contractual capacity). 'Know your customer' (KYC) requirements are important in ensuring that the firm can demonstrate it is managing the risks of financial crime. It is important that the client knows which legal entity is working on its behalf and in what capacity – particularly in cases where there are multiple group entities involved, or where the firm arranges custody as we have seen in previous chapters (and only provides execution or investment management). Such detail is critical in insolvency, or cases of contractual dispute, or if the client wishes to escalate a complaint against the relevant firm.

COBS requires certain disclosures be made to a prospective client when a firm is to perform regulatory business for that client, and CASS 9 includes a signpost reminding firms of the particular obligations relating to custody assets and client money.

To set out the contractual parties and respective obligations there will therefore be a formal client agreement – essentially a legal contract, often described as 'terms and conditions'. This should set out the obligations on each party to provide information or execute certain tasks within certain time periods in order that the client's instructions can be correctly carried out.

These terms and conditions will also enable the firm to document various factors we have explored during the workbook – such as the following:

- How will the client's assets be held? This will often include confirmation of the registration to be applied, and whether the assets will be pooled with assets of other clients – but will also confirm structural matters such as whether the firm is providing a custody service directly, or is 'arranging' for some other entity to directly provide the client with a custody service.
- What consents has the client given to the firm in respect of the business to be undertaken? Some consents will be specifically obtained in stand-alone documents (enabling each client to make their own decision about whether to grant the firm consent for a particular aspect of servicing). A possible example of such a consent would be the professional client opt-out, by which a particular client will agree to be treated as a professional client for its non-MiFID business and so receive a lesser level of CASS protection. Other consents might be written into the firm's terms and conditions as standard elements, though the firm's lawyers should always review such decisions to ensure that the clauses will be robust in the face of legal or regulatory scrutiny. Examples of consents that the firm might seek within its terms and conditions might include the use of a delivery versus payment (DvP) exemption when transacting in particular assets.
- Whether the firm is providing contractual settlement (and, if so, whether there is any limitation on the provision of contractual settlement, such as according to asset type) or will pass on actual settlement to its client. This is particularly important for the firm when establishing its CASS business processes: where the firm will give contractual settlement to the client, it should ensure that relevant sums are shown as 'due and payable' to the client on settlement date, and are paid to the client/into a client bank account (CBA) on that date, (rather than adopting a sequential processing approach by which the firm would only allocate the monies or assets that the firm has actually received). Remember that either approach can function under CASS; however, the firm must establish its CASS processes in the light of the client agreement being honoured.
- Whether the firm has unilateral power to amend the agreement (such as by advising the client of changes, to become effective after a certain number of days), or whether any change to the contract requires specific negotiation between the firm and each client. While the first approach enables the firm to maintain a standardised service across all clients, for some types of business such an approach might be too limiting, in which case the firm must take conscious and specific steps to ensure that it will support bespoke services, as this will affect the design and implementation of transaction processing and CASS controls within the firm. There are also certain elements which are required by the CASS rules to have the explicit agreement of the client, such as the use of TTCAs.
- The treatment of interest earned on client money balances should also be stated. A CASS 7 firm can apply interest to each client if it so chooses, though can alternatively disclose some different approach (particularly if the administration processes to correctly disaggregate interest earned on a centralised client money account would be disproportionate to the value of the interest expected). The firm might even arrange with its bank that no interest will be earned on client money balances. The contract with the client should clarify the position. If it is silent on this point, all interest received on client money balances must be paid to the clients.

End of Chapter Questions

Think of an answer for each question and refer to the appropriate section for confirmation

1.   What are three differences between the CASS treatment of a professional client compared with a
     retail client? *can notify rather than ask to hold in own name   in a termales*
     Answer reference: Section 1.1 *professional client opt out - no CASS protects*
     £100 ks to clarity

2.   CASS 7 will not apply to a firm holding or receiving client money in respect of the non-MiFID
     business of an affiliated company if any of three conditions are satisfied. What are those three
     conditions?   *atoas*
     Answer reference: Section 1.2

3.   How does CASS define a 'mandate', and what conditions must be satisfied?
     Answer reference: Section 2.1   *cold ability tradin dati mry /w t*

4.   Aside from maintaining a 'list of mandates', which four controls does CASS 8 require in respect of
     mandates?   *+ an   summy /procedures*
     Answer reference: Section 2.2   *internal audit   protecy pass bod*

5.   CASS 9 confirms two scenarios in which a firm must provide a statement detailing the client
     money and safe custody assets it holds for that client. What are these two scenarios?
     Answer reference: Section 3   *Ad hoc, annual*

6.   CASS 8 specifies five pieces of information that must be included on the firm's 'list of mandates'
     for each mandate received in non-written form. What are these five items?
     Answer reference: Section 2.2   *nature, purpose, obtained, name, when.*

7.   If a firm is holding assets within a jurisdiction that only supports registration in the name of the
     firm (rather than the name of the client, nominee, or other third party), how might the firm's
     actions differ depending on whether the client is a retail client or a professional client?
     Answer reference: Section 1.1   *inform vs reg t.*

8.   The terms & conditions should specify how the firm will treat any interest earned on client
     money balances. What treatment would be required for interest earned by a debt management
     firm?   *paid to clint*
     Answer reference: Section 4

9.   Why is it important for the terms and conditions to specify whether and how contractual
     settlement is being provided to the client?
     Answer reference: Section 4   *due + payable considerations*

10. What structural matters regarding the holding of safe custody assets should be set out in the
     terms and conditions?   *were held*
     Answer reference: Section 4

     GTO.

Glossary

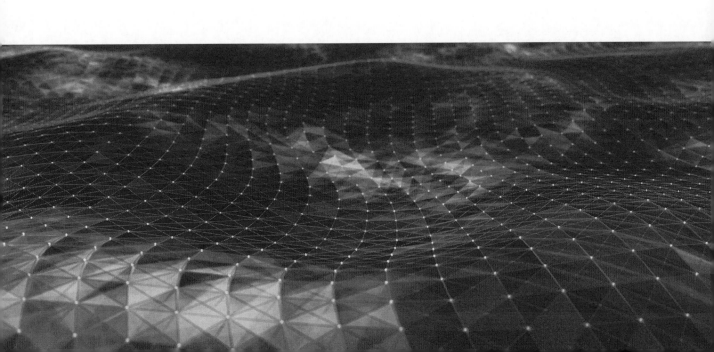

Agent

1. One party officially representing another, and acting on its behalf.
2. Role adopted when party to an investment transaction when the transaction will settle on the external market rather than within the firm (as distinct from a principal deal).

Auditor

An independent party, with expertise in the review of business operations and/or financial record-keeping, retained by a firm to ensure its operations are effective and accurate.

CASS

Abbreviated name for the Client Assets Sourcebook, part of the FCA Handbook of regulations.

CASS Resolution Pack

A set of documents that a firm must maintain to assist an insolvency practitioner understand and operate the CASS model if the firm were to become insolvent.

Client Asset

A term including both client money and safe custody assets.

Client Bank Account

A bank account opened by a firm specifically to hold client money rather than corporate money.

Client Money

Money of either of the following types: (a) money received by a firm from/for a client in respect of designated investment business (unless some exemption applies); or (b) money that the CASS rules specifically require a firm to segregate as client money (such as prudent segregation).

Client Money and Assets Return (CMAR)

A specific data return that regulated firms must submit to the FCA each month.

Client Transaction Account

An account opened with an exchange, clearing house, broker or counterparty for the purposes of settling transactions on behalf of clients.

COBS

The 'Conduct of Business' Sourcebook, part of the FCA Handbook.

COMP

The 'Compensation' Sourcebook; the part of the FCA Handbook dealing with FSCS.

Custodian

A regulated firm that specialises in the safeguarding and administration of transferable securities and other safe custody assets.

Deposit

A sum of money held by a bank or similar institution, and treated as a balance sheet item of the bank rather than a sum of client money held.

Designated Investment Business

A term that includes a wide range of specific activities that are subject to FCA authorisation and regulation, if performed for business purposes.

Due Diligence

A review process undertaken by a firm when selecting a bank or custodian etc. to appoint in respect of its holdings of client assets. Periodic reviews may also be performed.

Excess

The position where the actual money held or the client money resource calculated as part of an internal client money reconciliation exceeds the calculated requirement. CASS requires that the firm remove an excess sum from a client bank account.

Financial Conduct Authority (FCA)

The UK regulator responsible for the conduct of firms that look after client assets.

Financial Services Compensation Scheme (FSCS)

An industry-funded facility to compensate clients if a financial services firm fails to honour its obligations.

Firm

Term used to identify a legal company (or, for example, sole trader and partnership) that is authorised and regulated by the FCA to conduct designated investment business.

Individual Client Balance (ICB) Method

One of the standard methods of calculating the requirement in the internal client money reconciliation.

Net Negative Add-Back (NNAB) Method

One of the standard methods of internal client money reconciliation.

Nominee

A type of company that exists to hold assets on behalf of an operating company. As the nominee company has no direct business activities it should be secure against insolvency.

Primary Pooling Event (PPE)

Term used for a situation where a firm stops passing money through its existing pool of client money (such as following the firm's insolvency).

PRIN

The 'Principles for Business' Sourcebook, part of the FCA Handbook.

Principal

Role adopted when a firm deals for a client using the assets or money owned by the firm (as distinct from an agent deal).

Prudent Segregation

A specific process by which a firm can set aside a sum of corporate money to protect the client money pool against the risk of a potential shortfall.

Registration

The recording of ownership of an asset – particularly in the main register maintained by the issuer of an asset.

Regulated Activities

A specific list of financial service activities that may only be performed by a firm that is authorised by the FCA for that activity.

Requirement

The client money requirement is the figure calculated by a firm from its internal records indicating the amount of money that ought to have been segregated as at close of business on the prior business day. It will be compared against the resource.

Resource

The client money resource is the figure that the firm's internal records indicate is held in client accounts at third parties (such as banks) as at close of business on the prior business day. It will be compared against the requirement.

Safe Custody Asset

An asset held by a firm as part of providing a custody service to a client.

Secondary Pooling Event (SPE)

Term used for a situation where a firm no longer considers client money held at a given institution is available for use – requiring the firm to either resolve the shortfall created, or write down the entitlement of affected clients.

Segregation

The legal and physical separation between money and assets of the firm and the money and assets that the firm may hold on behalf of its clients.

Settlement

The exchange of assets and/or money at the conclusion of a financial services transaction.

Shortfall

The position where a CASS reconciliation or records check concludes that the amount held by/for the firm is less than the value owed to its clients.

Specified Investments

A list of asset types to which regulated activities relate. When applying for authorisation, each firm must record the types of specified investments that will be applicable to each regulated activity undertaken.

Standard Methods (of Internal Client Money Reconciliation)

A term used to describe either of two methods used to determine the firm's client money requirement for comparison against the client money resource. See also 'individual client balance method' and 'net negative add-back method'.

SUP

The 'Supervision' Sourcebook, part of the FCA Handbook dealing with the firm's interactions with FCA.

SYSC

The 'Senior Management Arrangements, Systems and Controls' Sourcebook, part of the FCA Handbook.

Transaction

An agreement to exchange a specific type and quantity of one asset (or money) for a specific type and quantity of another. A transaction will either be subject to the rules of the exchange on which it is executed, or the terms and conditions defining a service. Firms may therefore process a wide range of transactions – both internal and external.

Multiple Choice
Questions

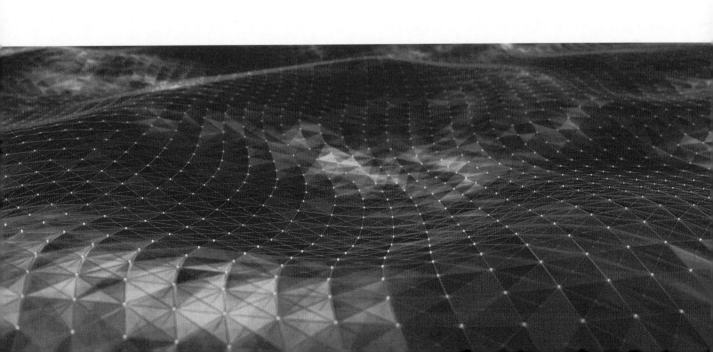

Multiple Choice Questions

The following questions have been compiled to reflect as closely as possible the exam standard that you will experience in your exam. Please note, however, they are not the CISI exam questions themselves.

1. Which of the following is true of the CASS 7 client money rules?

   A. They apply to money that the firm controls but does not hold

   B. Professional clients can opt out from CASS 7 protection if performing MiFID business with the firm

   C. Professional clients can opt out from CASS 7 protection if performing non-MiFID business with the firm

   D. External reconciliations must be performed at least weekly

2. Which of the following is not true in respect of firms that hold client money or have custody of client assets?

   A. The legal title of assets must always be registered in the name of a nominee controlled by the firm

   B. The firm remains responsible for assets held by a third party on the firm's behalf

   C. Bearer certificates held by the firm are subject to CASS 6

   D. Client bank accounts used to hold client money must be segregated from corporate accounts, with the firm acting as trustee

3. Which of the following best describes the overall aim and purpose of the client assets regime?

   A. To ensure firms have appropriate processes and procedures when holding client assets

   B. To ensure firms have adequate capital resources

   C. To ensure that clients are protected, particularly in the event of the firm's insolvency

   D. To ensure that firms have set aside sufficient assets to cover clients' liabilities

4. Which of the following is most true of a bare security interest?

   A. Legal ownership of the asset changes when the interest is created

   B. It is a form of collateral

   C. It establishes actions that will follow the default of a debtor party

   D. It enables the firm to enter into securities financing transactions

5. Which of the following events would the CASS rules not require the firm to notify the Financial Conduct Authority (FCA)?

   A. Failure to complete an external asset reconciliation

   B. Failure to effect prudent segregation where required by the firm's policy

   C. Material inaccuracy in the firm's records of safe custody assets held

   D. Making the required funding movement relating to a client money reconciliation discrepancy 24 hours after it was identified in the relevant reconciliation

6. Which of the following is a potential consequence if the firm chooses to offer contractual settlement when selling an asset for a client?

    A. Client money is 'due and payable' from firm to client on the trade date

    B. The firm will allocate settlement proceeds to the client regardless of whether an associated market transaction settles as scheduled

    C. The firm will only reduce the investor's asset position once the settlement proceeds have been received in the firm's client bank account (CBA)

    D. Prudent segregation is mandatory for such contracts

7. The 'Total Count Method' relates to what type of CASS control?

    A. Mandates

    B. Net negative add-back (NNAB)

    C. Internal system evaluation method (ISEM)

    D. Physical asset reconciliation

8. In which of the following would a CASS mandate be necessary?

    A. The firm is providing services of portfolio management in respect of assets held at its nominee

    B. A bank is making use of the banking exemption when holding client money

    C. The firm will collect periodic fees directly from the client's personal bank account

    D. The firm is the operator of a regulated collective investment scheme (CIS)

9. Which of the following would be treated as client money?

    A. Money received by a fund manager two days before the contractual settlement of a unit deal in a regulated collective investment scheme

    B. Money that is due and payable to the firm for periodic charges

    C. Commission rebates received by the firm but not yet contractually due to the client

    D. Money held on deposit in line with the banking exemption

10. Which of the following is true in respect of the client assets regime?

    A. The regime only applies to retail clients

    B. If the firm operates a 'designated bank account', that account will hold the money of all clients

    C. The UK operates a discretionary trust regime for firms holding client money

    D. The UK operates a statutory trust regime for firms holding client money

5/5.

8/10

11. If a firm chooses to use a non-standard method of internal client money reconciliation, which external entity must approve the approach?

    A. The Financial Conduct Authority (FCA)   *FCA notified.*

    B. The person responsible for CASS operational oversight

    C. The CASS auditor

    D. The Financial Reporting Council (FRC)

12. Which of the following is true in respect of the allocated but unclaimed custody assets requirements?

    A. The firm can dispose of the asset providing it has been held for at least six years

    B. The firm must use a search agency to demonstrate that it has tried to trace the client

    C. If the asset is valued at less than £25 the firm can simply transfer it to a corporate account

    D. CASS allows the firm to transfer the assets to a charity without an instruction from its client

13. A firm holds £28 of allocated but unclaimed client money for a retail investor. Which of the following must be true if the firm decides to pay this money away without an instruction from the client?

    A. The firm must have held the money for at least 12 years

    B. The firm must unconditionally undertake to pay to the client concerned the amount paid away to charity in the event of the client seeking to claim the balance in future

    C. The firms must use credit reference agencies and tracing agencies to trace the clients

    D. The individual performing the compliance oversight control function can approve the payment to the charity

14. Which of the following is true in relation to outsourcing arrangements in respect of a firm's client money and assets obligations?

    A. Firms that outsource client money activities do not require Financial Conduct Authority (FCA) permission to hold client money

    B. The third-party provider owes regulatory and contractual obligations to the firm

    C. The third-party provider enters into a relationship with the underlying clients of the firm

    D. The firm retains regulatory responsibility for the client money and assets requirements

15. Which of the following is true of client reporting obligations under CASS 9?

    A. The firm is not permitted to charge for providing an ad hoc statement

    B. The firm can charge a reasonable fee for the effort involved in providing a duplicate of a previous statement

    C. Duplicate statements must be provided within three business days of a request

    D. The report must only list those safe custody assets and client money balances that are held subject to CASS 6 and CASS 7 respectively

16. Which of the following is not a requirement placed on firms in respect of good governance and oversight?

    A. The firm must clearly identify and apportion responsibility among its directors

    B. The CASS operational oversight function must be performed by the individual who performs the regulatory compliance oversight function

    C. The compliance function must ensure it is monitoring the firm's activities against its regulatory obligations

    D. Firms are expected to maintain an effective compliance function which operates independently

17. Which of the following is true regarding client money?

    A. If the firm is a bank then it is not required to hold money as client money

    B. Client money can only be held at a central bank or a credit institution

    C. The alternative approach to segregating client money only applies to professional clients

    D. Client money cannot be held with a central bank

18. Which of the following statements could be true in respect of a CASS medium firm?

    A. An individual responsible for the oversight of CASS within the firm need not be personally approved by the Financial Conduct Authority (FCA)

    B. The highest total of client money held by the firm during a specific time period was £11 billion

    C. The client money and assets return (CMAR) must be undertaken on an annual basis

    D. The highest total of client custody assets held by the firm during a specific time period was £85 billion

19. Which of the following documents would provide information of a fine/regulatory sanction imposed by the Financial Conduct Authority (FCA)?

    A. Sourcebook

    B. Final notice

    C. Audit assurance report

    D. Regulated Activities Order

20. Which of the following is true in respect of the exemption rules that apply in relation to the custody rules?

    A. The exemptions apply in respect of professional clients only

    B. When a firm temporarily handles client custody assets it is not obliged to comply with Principle 10 (clients' assets)

    C. Before a firm makes use of the delivery versus payment (DvP) exemption it must obtain agreement from the client

    D. The DvP exemption only applies from one business day prior to the contractual settlement date

4/5   16/20

21. Which of the following is true in respect of the collateral rules?

    A. The rules apply to incoming European Economic Area (EEA) firms, in respect of passported services

    B. The rules only apply when the firm is acting for a retail client

    C. The rules apply even when a firm only has a bare interest in client assets

    D. The purpose of the collateral rules is to provide adequate protection of assets when the firm is engaged in transactions requiring collateral

22. Which of the following is true of the banking exemption?

    A. The exemption applies only to European Economic Area (EEA) and third-country banks

    B. Banks have to apply to the Bank of England for the exemption

    C. Under the banking exemption, a bank is not permitted to hold more than 20% of funds with a group-related entity

    D. Banks need to disclose and explain to clients that their cash will be held by the firm as 'banker' rather than as 'client money'

23. Which of the following is most true of the 'normal approach' to segregating client money?

    A. The firm must receive the money from the client into the firm's account and then transfer it to a client bank account at a credit institution

    B. Client money can only be held at a central bank or credit institution

    C. Firms must undertake annual reviews of each financial institution used to deposit client money

    D. The client must pay their money directly to a client bank account of the firm, opened at a third party

24. Which of the following is a specified duty of the CASS operational oversight officer?

    A. Highlighting to the regulator where the firm has discrepancies in its reconciliation processes for client money

    B. Approving the firm's CASS audit report

    C. Agreeing on the method of internal reconciliations

    D. Submitting the firm's client money and assets return (CMAR)

25. Which of the following best describes the CASS 7 obligations relating to bank interest earned?

    A. The trust acknowledgement letter prevents a client bank account (CBA) from earning interest

    B. The firm must pay retail clients their share of any interest earned on client money balances

    C. The firm must pay all clients their share of any interest earned on client money balances

    D. The firm can advise the client what (if any) interest the client will receive

26. What is the main purpose of a client bank account (CBA) acknowledgement letter?

    A. It provides the bank's confirmation of money it has placed with itself

    B. It is a one-way confirmation from the firm that funds deposited with the bank are treated as client money

    C. It requires the bank to recognise that the money is client money and that there is no right of set-off in respect of any sum owed to it

    D. It enables the CASS oversight function to prevent error and control the parties holding client money of the firm

27. Which of the following is correct in respect of the records and internal control requirements in relation to mandates?

    A. The mandate must be part of the client agreement

    B. Firms need to only retain records of the mandate for one year following it ceasing to exist for non-MiFID business   MIFID is 5 .

    C. The mandate list must be maintained by the CASS operational oversight function

    D. No records are required to be maintained of non-European Economic Area (EEA) clients

28. Which of the following is true in respect of the client money and assets return (CMAR)?

    A. Large CASS firms must submit a CMAR every six months

    B. Small CASS firms must submit a CMAR each year ?

    C. Safe custody asset reconciliation items of less than 30 days are not included in the CMAR

    D. CMARs must be submitted on the first business day of the month of submission

29. Which of the following is true in respect of a firm holding client money and safeguarding client assets?

    A. Firms need to obtain permission from the Bank of England, aside from any Financial Conduct Authority (FCA) permission obtained

    B. The FCA would authorise the firm for both activities

    C. An FCA-regulated firm needs to hold its client money in deposit accounts at the Bank of England

    D. The firm is automatically classified as a CASS Large Firm

30. Which of the following is true in relation to client asset protection?

    A. The firm's CASS auditor must provide an annual assurance report to the regulator

    B. Auditors must provide a 'reasonable assurance report' to a firm that did not hold client money or assets during the period

    C. The Client Assets Sourcebook dictates the firms that can hold client money

    D. The audit report must be submitted within two months of the period ending

3/5

22/50

178

31. Which of the following is true in respect of securities financing transactions?

    A. Firms do not need written client consent to enter into securities financing transactions in respect of client custody assets

    B. Firms are required to hold adequate records that identify which clients have given consent and the assets that will be used for lending

    C. The use of a retail client's assets is not permitted, unless they opt out of the client money and assets rules

    D. The firm must record the corporate assets it allocates to the client for this purpose

32. Which of the following is true of CASS requirements for firms when selecting third parties to deposit client money with?

    A. Only banks incorporated in the UK may hold client money on behalf of firms

    B. Firms must limit the amount of money held with group entities to no more than 20% of all the client money held by the firm

    C. Firms must undertake annual reviews of the financial institutions with which they deposit client money

    D. No more than 20% of the total of all the client money held by the firm can be deposited with a single financial institution

33. Which of the following is true in respect of liens?

    A. A lien is the right given to another by the owner of property to secure a debt

    B. A lien arises where two parties dispute control of a specific asset

    C. When a client transfers assets to a firm then a lien is placed over the assets by the firm

    D. Firms cannot prevent liens being applied by third parties in jurisdictions outside the European Economic Area (EEA)

34. Which of the following is true in respect of the CASS resolution pack?

    A. A firm that does not have permission to hold or control client money and that does have permission to arrange safeguarding and administration of assets need not maintain a CASS resolution pack

    B. The CASS resolution pack must be provided to the Financial Conduct Authority (FCA) annually

    C. Firms must be able to retrieve documents required within 12 hours

    D. Firms must be able to retrieve documents required within 24 hours

35. Which of the following best describes the main purpose of the internal client money reconciliation?

    A. To support the Financial Reporting Council (FRC) standard audit tests

    B. To ensure that discrepancies in the firm's records are investigated and resolved

    C. To evidence the firm's internal oversight of any external party holding client money

    D. To ensure that third parties are holding funds deposited with them as client money

36. Which of the following is true in respect of the permission to safeguard and administer assets?

   A. A firm is not permitted to undertake the safeguarding and administering of assets until it has been granted the relevant Financial Conduct Authority (FCA) permission

   B. The Prudential Regulation Authority (PRA) authorisation team approves all applications, even from FCA-only regulated entities

   C. A firm with the permission to accept deposits would be permitted to provide safeguarding and administration of assets

   D. A bank making use of the 'banking exemption' does not need to apply for permission to safeguard client assets

37. Which of the following is true in respect of a firm depositing assets with third parties?

   A. Firms must undertake annual reviews of the third parties

   B. The initial assessment of the third party must be submitted to the Financial Conduct Authority (FCA)

   C. The initial assessment record must be retained for a period of five years

   D. In some markets, the assets might be registered in the third party's name, providing the firm has notified its client in writing to that effect

38. What is the main purpose of the ICRC?

   A. To ensure compliance with regulatory requirements

   B. To ensure the firm's operational and risk management practices are appropriate

   C. To update the firm's records to match the statements of assets provided by third parties holding clients' assets

   D. To assess the accuracy of the firm's records of safe custody asset positions

39. What is the current maximum Financial Services Compensation Scheme (FSCS) compensation available for investment business done with a single firm?

   A. £100,000 of all losses

   B. £100,000 for non-delivered assets or guaranteed returns

   C. £85,000 of all losses

   D. £85,000 for non-delivered assets or guaranteed returns

40. Which of the following is true of the standard methods of internal client money reconciliation?

   A. Any discrepancy between the client money resource and client money requirement needs to be investigated once discovered, and action taken that same day to resolve it

   B. The reconciliation is completed using amounts/values provided from third-party statements

   C. Reconciliations must be carried out at least weekly

   D. Firms must obtain approval from the Financial Conduct Authority (FCA) prior to using these methods of reconciliation

41. Which of the following is true in respect of a firm holding safe custody assets?

    A. CASS requires the external custody reconciliations to be completed each day

    B. Firms must investigate and resolve external discrepancies within seven days from identifying the issue

    C. The Financial Conduct Authority (FCA) must be notified immediately if the firm's internal records are materially out of date or inaccurate

    D. Firms do not cover any shortfall resulting from discrepancies identified in an internal reconciliation

42. Which of the following is true of the client money distribution requirements?

    A. A secondary pooling event is due to the failure of the firm

    B. Client money distribution requirements only apply to retail clients

    C. Following a primary pooling event (PPE), new money received from a client for an existing contract should be banked to the original intended client money pool

    D. A PPE occurs only upon insolvency of the firm

43. If a paragraph within the Financial Conduct Authority (FCA) Handbook is denoted by letter 'E', what type of text does it concern?

    A. Elective provision

    B. Evidential provision

    C. European provision

    D. External provision

44. What is the minimum frequency required by CASS for a firm to perform an external custody reconciliation?

    A. Daily

    B. Weekly

    C. Monthly

    D. No minimum frequency is stated

45. Which of the following is true in respect of a firm's CASS audit report?

    A. The auditor must provide the report to the FCA within four months from the end of the period covered

    B. The auditor's report must be approved by the firm's CASS operational oversight officer

    C. A copy of the CASS RP must accompany the audit report

    D. If the auditor will not be able to meet the reporting deadline, the firm must advise the FCA

46. Which of the following is true in relation to a firm domiciled in the EU which wants to perform investment activity within the UK?

    A. The firm need not be authorised by the FCA, and will continue to comply with the client asset rules in its home EU State

    B. The firm need not be authorised by the FCA, but must comply with CASS rules

    C. If the firm chooses to be authorised by the FCA it must comply with the CASS rules

    D. The firm must become authorised by the FCA and comply with the CASS rules

47. Which of the following best describes the client assets regime's interaction with the Financial Conduct Authority (FCA) objectives?

    A. Firms secure an appropriate degree of protection for consumers

    B. Firms must protect and enhance the integrity of the financial system

    C. There must be effective competition in the interests of customers

    D. Consumers get financial services that meet their needs from firms that they can trust

48. Which of the following best describes a firm's responsibility for resolving a discrepancy identified in an external custody reconciliation?

    A. The missing assets must be applied to the account on the day the discrepancy is identified

    B. The firm must instigate an asset purchase in the market on the day the reconciliation is identified, but need take no other action

    C. If the firm cannot resolve a shortfall using assets, it should segregate an equivalent value of cash until the discrepancy can be resolved

    D. If the firm considers that the discrepancy arose because of an error by a third party, the firm must not cover the shortfall

49. Which of the following is true in respect of trust law and applies to firms holding client money?

    A. Trust law only applies to retail clients

    B. The signed acknowledgement letter returned to the firm evidences that a client bank account (CBA) is protected under trust law

    C. Trust law only applies to UK banks

    D. Legal agreements need not be entered into for professional clients

50. CASS defines two methods by which a firm can complete an internal custody record check (ICRC). One is the internal custody reconciliation method; what is the other method?

    A. Total count method

    B. Internal system evaluation method

    C. The standard method

    D. Individual client balance method

5/5

39/50

pass 78+

Answers to Multiple Choice Questions

1.   **C**   **Chapter 9, Section 1.1**

For non-MiFID business only, the 'professional client opt-out' enables a firm to allow a professional client to choose whether their money should be handled as client money or not.

2.   **A**   **Chapter 5, Section 2.2**

Assets could be registered in the name of the individual underlying client, or a nominee company. In some international situations, CASS permits that assets might be registered in the name of a third party or the firm itself.

3.   **C**   **Chapter 1, Section 1.1**

It is important that consumers can be confident that a regulated firm will take good care of any money or assets it holds on their behalf, and the Client Assets Sourcebook sets out the Financial Conduct Authority's (FCA's) requirements on regulated firms in this regard. While CASS is important in how a relevant firm runs its business at all times, the potential risks for a consumer are perhaps best illustrated by considering the potential consequences if a firm was to become insolvent while holding assets of its clients.

4.   **C**   **Chapter 5, Section 4.2**

A bare security interest is not therefore an example of 'collateral', because the asset does not change owner unless the terms are triggered on a default. Creating the bare security interest does not itself require any transfer of ownership/registration; it only creates a legal understanding that if the debtor party defaults on its payment, the full ownership of the asset concerned would transfer to the creditor party.

5.   **B**   **Chapter 7, Section 1.2**

Failing to apply the firm's prudent segregation policy is not a notifiable event under CASS.

6.   **B**   **Chapter 1, Section 2.4**

'Contractual settlement' means that the firm honours the terms of the original contract. For a sold asset, the firm would record the cash as being available for the client's use with effect from the contractual settlement date of the transaction, regardless of any upstream failed settlement. The firm portrays to its client that the settlement was completed as intended.

7.   **D**   **Chapter 6, Section 2.1**

CASS offers two methods that can be used when performing a physical asset reconciliation: the Total Count Method and the Rolling Stock Method.

8.   **C**   **Chapter 9, Section 2.1**

CASS defines a 'mandate' as being 'any means' that would enable the firm to control a client's assets (or liabilities) held elsewhere – providing that five specific conditions are satisfied. For example, if a firm receives its customer's debit card details or bank account details (both of which would enable the firm to send instructions to collect the client's money) those would be 'means' in the context of CASS 8.

9.　　　A　　　　　Chapter 3, Section 7.2

While an authorised fund manager can receive settlement monies into a corporate bank account, if the client's money is received more than one day prior to contractual settlement date the sum must be segregated as client money.

10.　　　D　　　　　Chapter 1, Section 3.3

The client assets regime applies to both professional and retail clients. A designated client bank account (CBA) is used to hold the money of only certain of the firm's clients.

The UK operates a statutory 'trust' regime whereby client money is held by firms separately from its own money in designated client money bank accounts – so as to distinguish it from the firm's own money.

11.　　　C　　　　　Chapter 4, Section 4

If a firm decides to use a non-standard method, that method must receive prior approval from the firm's auditor. While the decision will be notified to the Financial Conduct Authority (FCA), the FCA does not give approval.

12.　　　D　　　　　Chapter 5, Section 3.5

CASS permits a firm to dispose of assets if there has been no contact/instructions received from the client in the last 12 years, either transferring the asset to a registered charity or selling the asset and paying the proceeds to the registered charity. The following conditions must be met:

- The firm has held the safe custody assets for at least 12 years.
- The firm can demonstrate that it has taken all reasonable steps to trace the client concerned and return the safe custody assets.
- The firm must unconditionally undertake to pay the client the value of the assets at the time they were paid away if the client subsequently claims them.

13.　　　B　　　　　Chapter 3, Section 3.7

A firm may pay away to a registered charity, of its choice, a client money balance which is allocated to a client if it has held the balance concerned for at least six years following the last movement on the client's account and has demonstrated that it has taken reasonable steps to trace the client concerned and to return the balance. For larger sums (above £25 for a retail client, or above £100 for other clients) the firm must make an unconditional undertaking to pay the sum to the client if so requested in the future

14.　　　D　　　　　Chapter 7, Section 3.2

The firm retains full regulatory responsibility for the administrative tasks undertaken by the outsourced service provider.

15.　　　B　　　　　Chapter 9, Section 3.1

CASS 9 allows the firm to receive a fee for the additional effort, providing that fee reasonably corresponds to the costs incurred by the firm. (Note: there is no equivalent ability to recover costs for issuing the original annual statement of client money and safe custody assets held.)

CASS 9 also highlights that any statement should clarify which of the money or assets listed are held subject to the respective CASS 6 and CASS 7 rules and which are not.

16.   B   Chapter 7, Section 2.1

A CASS firm must identify a director or senior manager to be responsible for CASS operational oversight. While the Financial Conduct Authority (FCA) would not therefore specifically approve the individual for this oversight function, the individual would already have been approved by the FCA for a senior manager function and so have sufficient seniority within the firm to exercise this additional duty.

17.   A   Chapter 2, Section 2.3

A credit institution or approved bank may hold money as a deposit rather than client money (referred to as 'the banking exemption').

18.   D   Chapter 2, Section 3.2

For a firm to be classified as a CASS medium firm it would hold between £1 million and £1 billion in client money and between £10 million and £100 billion in client custody assets.

The client money and assets return (CMAR) must be completed monthly for large and medium CASS firms.

19.   B   Chapter 8, Section 4.1

The Financial Conduct Authority (FCA) publishes details of all regulatory sanctions it issues. Such 'final notices' provide details of the failures observed, and in the case of CASS events, the final notice will usually indicate the value of client assets that were exposed to potential loss as a result of the failures concerned.

20.   C   Chapter 5, Section 3.4.1

The delivery versus payment (DvP) exemption in CASS 6 allows a firm a three- to four-day window during which the asset need not be treated as a CASS 6 asset. The client concerned must have provided written agreement confirming that the firm may apply the exemption.

21.   D   Chapter 5, Section 4.3

Where a firm wishes to use the client's assets as collateral it must ensure that it obtains from its client a 'right to use' that client's assets for that purpose. CASS 3 confirms that in such a case exercising the 'right to use' an asset equates to a change in legal ownership of that asset, such that it belongs to the firm rather than the client. Such an event must be clearly recorded in the firm's books and records.

22.   D   Chapter 2, Section 2.3

A bank making use of the exemption must disclose to clients the fact that the money will be held as banker and is not protected under the client money rules.

23.   D   Chapter 3, Section 2.1

The normal approach is where client money received is paid directly into a client bank account (CBA) at a relevant financial institution, rather than being first received into the firm's own account and then segregated.

While firms would be required to undertake periodic reviews of a credit institution and/or bank with which they deposit client money, CASS does not require that such reviews be annual.

24.   D   Chapter 7, Section 2

The role/responsibility of the CASS oversight function is to oversee the operational effectiveness of the firm's systems and controls that are designed to achieve compliance with CASS; report to the firm's governing body in respect of that oversight; and complete/submit the client money and assets return (CMAR) to the Financial Conduct Authority (FCA).

25.   D   Chapter 3, Section 3.5.2

CASS 7 requires that any interest earned on client money held for a client should be paid to that client – unless the firm has notified the client in writing that a different approach will be taken. Where a firm does choose to effect an interest allocation (rather than notifying the clients that any such interest will be claimed instead by the firm), it is common for the firm to simply specify a rate of interest which it will pay, and to effect its own daily accrual based on its own ledger of client entitlement.

26.   C   Chapter 3, Section 3.3

The firm sends to the bank a signed acknowledgement letter, and the bank will countersign the letter and return it to the firm. This provides the firm with documented evidence that both the bank and the firm have acknowledged that the money held in that account is legally segregated as relating to the firm's clients.

27.   B   Chapter 9, Section 2.2

A firm should continue to ensure that it can demonstrate that the mandate had been subject to the correct controls for a period of at least one year. For MiFID business this period increases to at least five years.

28.   C   Chapter 7, Section 2.3

The client money and assets return (CMAR) includes safe custody asset reconciliation unresolved items by age: 30–59 days; 60–89 days; and over 90 days.

29.   B   Chapter 2, Section 2.1

Both these business activities would be included in the Financial Conduct Authority (FCA) regulatory permissions obtained by the firm.

30.   **A**   **Chapter 7, Section 4.1**

Regulated firms are required to retain the services of a CASS auditor. Where the firm holds client assets or client money a 'reasonable assurance' review would be performed, and a 'limited assurance' review performed where the firm states that no client money or client assets were held. One obligation of the CASS auditor is to submit an annual CASS auditor's report to the Financial Conduct Authority (FCA), commenting upon the firm's CASS controls.

31.   **B**   **Chapter 5, Section 4.3**

A firm that intends to use the client's assets as collateral for a securities financing transaction must ensure that its client provides a 'right to use' the relevant assets for that purpose.

32.   **B**   **Chapter 4, Section 1.1**

Firms must limit the amount of funds that they deposit or hold with a relevant group entity or combination of such entities so that the value of those funds does not at any point in time exceed 20% of the total of all the client money held by firms in their client bank accounts.

Firms must periodically assess the financial institutions that they have placed client money with, though CASS does not require such assessments be performed annually.

33.   **A**   **Chapter 5, Section 4.2**

A lien is a right granted over an asset to secure some future payment (or the fulfilment of some other type of obligation between the parties). A key feature of a lien is that the asset remains the legal property of the first party until that first party fails to fulfil their obligations under the contract concerned – at which point full ownership of the asset passes to the second party in settlement of that obligation.

34.   **A**   **Chapter 8, Section 3**

A CASS resolution pack (CASS RP) must be maintained by firms that hold client assets/money. A firm with permissions only to 'arrange' safeguarding and administration will not itself hold client money or safe custody assets.

35.   **B**   **Chapter 4, Section 3.1**

The internal client money reconciliation ensures that the firm's client ledger and bank ledger are aligned with each other, and that any differences are identified, understood, and promptly resolved.

36.   **A**   **Chapter 2, Section 2**

The Financial Services and Markets Act 2000 (FSMA) is the primary legislation that sets out the regulatory structures for UK financial services. It is supported by various other legal materials, including the Regulated Activities Order (RAO), which establishes the specific types of activity that can only be performed by a firm holding the relevant Financial Conduct Authority (FCA) authorisation.

37. **D** **Chapter 5, Section 2.2**

The firm might use the services of a third party to hold the assets (without utilising a nominee company). The firm must have assessed whether proceeding in the proposed way remains in the client's best interests, and the firm must notify the client in writing that proceeding will mean that the assets will not be protected in the usual manner.

38. **D** **Chapter 6, Section 2.2**

The internal custody record check (ICRC) can be achieved by either of two methods: internal custody reconciliation method or the internal system evaluation method (ISEM). Both should enable the firm to identify errors within its internal records of safe custody assets held.

39. **D** **Chapter 8, Section 1.2**

For investment activity, the Financial Services Compensation Scheme (FSCS) protects 100% of the value of the assets lost, up to a maximum of £85,000 per person, per firm.

Note, the compensation relates to any failure by the firm to deliver assets that should have been held, or provide any investment return that was specifically guaranteed. Losses due to the reduction in market value of the investments are not protected by FSCS.

40. **A** **Chapter 4, Section 4**

The standard methods of internal client money reconciliation determine the calculation of the client money resource and client money requirement each day. Any discrepancy between the client money resource and client money requirement needs to be investigated once discovered, and action taken that same day to resolve it.

41. **C** **Chapter 7, Section 1.2**

CASS 6 requires a firm to notify the Financial Conduct Authority (FCA) if its internal records and accounts of safe custody assets are materially out-of-date, or inaccurate/invalid, to the extent that the firm cannot distinguish assets held for different clients.

42. **C** **Chapter 8, Section 2.2**

CASS notes that any money received after the primary pooling event (PPE) which relates to investment business contracted prior to the PPE should continue to be accepted by the firm within the pre-PPE client money pool.

43. **B** **Chapter 2, Section 1.3**

'E' denotes an 'evidential provision'. This is a specific form of guidance which produces a regulatory 'safezone'. Where a firm can show it has satisfied an evidential provision, that fact is deemed to demonstrate compliance with the associated rule (where normal 'guidance' paragraphs will usually still leave some space for interpretation).

44.   **C**   **Chapter 6, Section 2.1**

CASS requires a firm to undertake this reconciliation 'as regularly as necessary', though the period between external custody reconciliations must not exceed one month.

45.   **A**   **Chapter 7, Section 4.1**

The auditor's assurance report must be delivered to the Financial Conduct Authority (FCA) within four months from the end of the period covered.

46.   **D**   **Chapter 2, Section 4.2**

Passports are not however applicable where an EEA-regulated firm wants to offer services in a country outside the EEA. In such cases, full domestic authorisation would be required, and the relevant rules therefore applied.

47.   **A**   **Chapter 1, Section 1.1**

The Financial Conduct Authority's (FCA)'s strategic objective is supported by three operational objectives – one of which is to make sure that firms secure an appropriate degree of protection for consumers.

48.   **C**   **Chapter 6, Section 2.3**

The firm may not be able to apply shares on the same day (as market trades may need to be traded and settled). If the shares cannot be applied, the relevant sum of corporate money can be segregated to cover the shortfall. Even if the firm considers that a third party's error was the cause of the shortfall, the firm should still consider whether a shortfall has arisen.

49.   **B**   **Chapter 3, Section 3.3**

An acknowledgement letter is a legal document, using wording specified in the CASS rules, which evidences the nature and purpose of the trust being established over the client money.

50.   **B**   **Chapter 6, Section 2.2**

CASS identifies two ways in which the internal custody record check (ICRC) might be achieved: The internal custody reconciliation method and the internal system evaluation method (ISEM).

Syllabus Learning Map

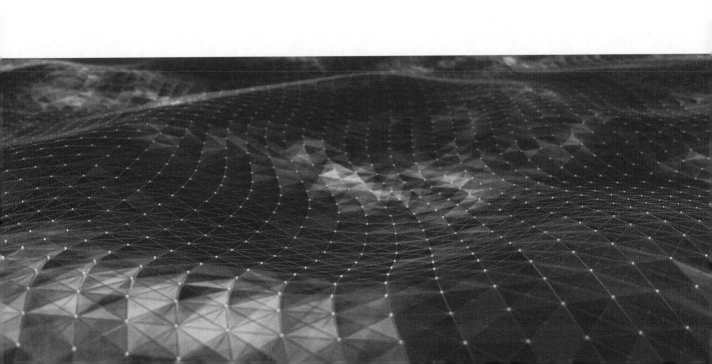

Syllabus Unit/ Element		Chapter/ Section
Element 1	**Fundamentals of Client Money and Assets**	**Chapter 1**
1.1	**Fundamentals of Client Money and Assets** On completion, the candidate should:	
1.1.1	Understand the objectives of the UK CASS regime and the interaction with the FCA's statutory objectives	1
1.1.2	Know the importance of legal entity separation	1.2
1.2	**Legal Contracts and Relationships** On completion, the candidate should:	
1.2.1	Understand the importance of client agreements	2.1
1.2.2	Understand the difference between contractual and actual settlement and the key implications for client assets segregation: • transfer and other settlement systems	2.4
1.3	**Looking after Assets for Investors** On completion, the candidate should:	
1.3.1	Know that the UK operates a trust regime and other types of regime (agency and custodial regimes)	3
1.3.2	Understand the fundamental concepts of trust law, including the concept of fiduciary duty, statutory trust and pollution of the trust	3
1.3.3	Know how legal title is registered and recorded	3
Element 2	**Regulatory Structures**	**Chapter 2**
2.1	**The Financial Conduct Authority and its Rules** On completion, the candidate should:	
2.1.1	Understand the meaning and purpose of the elements of the FCA Handbook that are relevant to client assets protection, including: • the FCA Principles for Business (PRIN) • Senior Management Arrangements, Systems and Controls (organisational arrangements) (SYSC) • CASS Sourcebook • Conduct of Business Sourcebook (COBS) • Supervision (SUP) • Compensation (COMP)	1
2.2	**FCA Authorisation and Permitted Business** On completion, the candidate should:	
2.2.1	Understand the scope of regulated activities which could give rise to client assets	2
2.2.2	Know the geographical application of CASS rules	2

Syllabus Unit/ Element		Chapter/ Section
2.2.3	Know which permissions could give rise to client money obligations	2
2.2.4	Know how permission to hold client money is granted	2
2.2.5	Know the difference between holding client money and deposit-taking	2
2.2.6	Understand the application of the banking exemption	2
2.3	**Roles and Responsibilities** **On completion, the candidate should:**	
2.3.1	Know the roles and responsibilities of the following in relation to client assets protection: • the FCA • authorised firms that hold or control client money or assets • SMF Prescribed Responsibility 'z' • auditors	3
2.3.2	Know the classifications of authorised firms as per CASS 1A	3.2
2.4	**International Considerations** **On completion, the candidate should:**	
2.4.1	Understand the general requirements of MiFID as they relate to client assets protection	4.1
2.4.2	Know the general requirements of the Insurance Distribution Directive relating to client money	4.1

Element 3	Client Money Fundamentals	Chapter 3
3.1	**Segregation of Client Money** **On completion, the candidate should:**	
3.1.1	Understand the normal approach to client money segregation	2.1
3.2	**Client Bank Accounts** **On completion, the candidate should:**	
3.2.1	Know where, and into which types of account, client money can be deposited	3
3.2.2	Know the definitions of general client bank accounts and designated client bank accounts	3
3.2.3	Know the function of an acknowledgement letter	3.3
3.2.4	Be able to apply the requirements of CASS to completing an acknowledgement letter, using the FCA templates	3.3
3.2.5	Understand when money becomes client money, including the treatment of interest and commission	3.4

Syllabus Unit/ Element		Chapter/ Section
3.2.6	Understand when money ceases to be client money	3.6
3.2.7	Know the treatment of allocated but unclaimed client money	3.7
3.2.8	Know how to treat mixed remittance	3.8
3.2.9	Know the requirements around client money held in different currencies	3.9
3.3	**Client Transaction Accounts** **On completion, the candidate should:**	
3.3.1	Know the difference between client bank accounts and client transaction accounts and the different treatment of each	4
3.4	**'The Alternative Approach' to Client Money Segregation** **On completion, the client should:**	
3.4.1	Understand the alternative approach to client money segregation and the approaches to managing risk arising from its use	5
3.5	**Other Money Segregated as Client Money** **On completion, the client should:**	
3.5.1	Know the rules around allocation of client money, including unidentified and unallocated amounts	6.1
3.5.2	Understand the concept of prudent segregation	6.2
3.5.3	Know the record-keeping requirements around prudent segregation	6.2
3.6	**Exemptions** **On completion, the candidate should:**	
3.6.1	Understand the use of exemptions available within the client money rules	7

Element 4	**Controls over Client Money (CASS 7)**	**Chapter 4**
4.1	**Controls over the Selection of a Bank**	
4.1.1	Understand firms' responsibilities in respect of bank selection, appointment, and review	1
4.1.2	Understand the client money diversification rules	1.1
4.2	**Client Money Books and Records** **On completion, the candidate should:**	
4.2.1	Know which books and records should be maintained and their function	2
4.3	**CASS 7 Reconciliations** **On completion, the candidate should:**	

Syllabus Unit/ Element		Chapter/ Section
4.3.1	Understand the purposes of the internal and external client money reconciliations	3
4.3.2	Know how often the client money reconciliations must be performed	3
4.3.3	Be able to apply the external reconciliation requirements	3.2
4.4	**The Standard Methods of Client Money Reconciliation** **On completion, the candidate should:**	
4.4.1	Understand the difference between the standard methods and non-standard methods of internal client money reconciliation	4
4.4.2	Be able to apply the standard methods of internal client money reconciliation	4
4.4.3	Understand how to deal with reconciliation discrepancies	4
4.4.4	Know what the margined transaction requirement is	4.2.5

Element 5	Safe Custody Fundamentals (CASS 6)	Chapter 5
5.1	**Segregation of Safe Custody Assets** **On completion, the candidate should:**	
5.1.1	Understand the requirements for the segregation of safe custody assets	
5.2	**Depositing Assets with Third Parties** **On completion, the candidate should:**	
5.2.1	Know the obligations created by the permissions: • safeguarding and administration of assets (without arranging) • arranging safeguarding and administration	2
5.2.2	Understand the different legal obligations that arise in respect of custody relationships	2
5.2.3	Understand the implications and risks of intragroup models and third party appointments	2
5.2.4	Understand firms' responsibilities in respect of the selection, appointment, and review of a third-party custodian	2
5.2.5	Understand the rules concerning depositing assets outside of the UK	2.2
5.2.6	Understand the requirements for third-party custody agreements	
5.3	**Exemptions** **On completion, the candidate should:**	
5.3.1	Understand the use of exemptions available within the custody rules	

Syllabus Unit/ Element		Chapter/ Section
5.4	**Types of Securities Interest** **On completion, the candidate should:**	
5.4.1	Understand the impact of legal arrangements on the custody rules (CASS 6): • bare security interests • right to use clauses/rehypothecation • title transfer collateral arrangements (TTCA)	1
5.4.2	Understand when the collateral rules (CASS 3) apply	1
5.4.3	Understand when a firm can enter into securities financing transactions in respect of client assets	1
5.4.4	Know the circumstances in which liens may be granted over client assets	1

Element 6	**Controls over Safe Custody Assets (CASS 6)**	**Chapter 6**
6.1	**Custody Books and Records** **On completion, the candidate should:**	
6.1.1	Know which books and records should be maintained and the function of each	3.1
6.2	**CASS 6 Reconciliations and Record Checks** **On completion, the candidate should:**	
6.2.1	Understand the purpose of the external custody reconciliations, physical asset reconciliations and internal custody record checks	3.2
6.2.2	Understand how to treat reconciliation discrepancies	3.4
6.2.3	Understand firms' obligations in relation to shortfalls	3.4
6.2.4	Know how often the reconciliations must be carried out	3.5

Element 7	**Governance and Oversight**	**Chapter 6**
7.1	**Organisational Arrangements** **On completion, the candidate should:**	
7.1.1	Know the rules on organisational arrangements as set out in CASS 6 and CASS 7	1.1
7.1.2	Know firms' obligations to notify the FCA of breaches in accordance with CASS 6 and 7	1.1
7.2	**CASS Oversight within a Regulated Firm** **On completion, the candidate should:**	
7.2.1	Understand the role responsible for CASS operational oversight within a firm, and its relationship with Prescribed Responsibility 'z'	2

Syllabus Unit/ Element		Chapter/ Section
7.2.2	Know the requirements for the content and submission of the Client Money and Assets Return (CMAR)	2.3
7.3	**Corporate Governance Arrangements** **On completion, the candidate should:**	
7.3.1	Understand the elements of good oversight, including appropriate governance, training, compliance, risk management, and internal audit	3.1
7.3.2	Understand the firm's oversight responsibilities in respect of outsourcing arrangements	3.2
7.4	**The CASS Audit and Assurance Standard** **On completion, the candidate should:**	
7.4.1	Know the duty of the CASS auditor to submit a client assets report	4
7.4.2	Know the difference between a reasonable assurance engagement and a limited assurance engagement and when these apply	4
7.4.3	Know the content, format, and submission deadline of the client assets report and be aware of the FRC standard that applies	4
7.4.4	Know the role of the Financial Reporting Council (FRC) in respect of the client asset assurance standard	4

Element 8	When Problems Arise....	Chapter 8
8.1	**Financial Services Compensation Scheme (FSCS)** **On completion, the candidate should:**	
8.1.1	Know in what circumstances the Financial Services Compensation Scheme will pay compensation, and how much	1
8.2	**Client Money Distribution and Transfer (CASS 7a)** **On completion, the candidate should:**	
8.2.1	Know the definitions of a primary pooling event and a secondary pooling event	2
8.2.2	Know how client money is treated in a primary pooling event	2
8.2.3	Know how client money is treated in a secondary pooling event	2
8.3	**CASS Resolution Pack (CASS 10)**	
8.3.1	Understand the purpose of a CASS resolution pack	3
8.3.2	Know the contents of and the requirements for the updating a CASS resolution pack	3

Syllabus Unit/ Element		Chapter/ Section
8.3.3	Understand the time frames for retrieval of this information and what this means for operational support	3
8.3.4	Know firms' obligations to notify the FCA of breaches in accordance with CASS 10	3
8.4	**Consequences of Regulatory Failure**	
8.4.1	Know the historical background, including key cases that have shaped the regime	4

Element 9	The Client	Chapter 9
9.1	**Client Types and CASS Exemptions**	
9.1.1	Know the application of the client money rules to: • professional clients (and the professional client opt-out) • affiliates • credit institutions and approved banks	1
9.2	**Mandates (CASS 8)**	
9.2.1	Know the definition of a mandate	2
9.2.2	Understand the circumstances that may give rise to a mandate	2
9.2.3	Know what records and internal controls have to be maintained in respect of mandates	2
9.3	**Client Reporting (CASS 9)**	
9.3.1	Know the obligations regarding reporting and information to clients contained in CASS 9	3
9.4	**Client Relationships, Contracts and Agreements**	
9.4.1	Understand the purpose of client agreements	4
9.4.2	Know the different types of agreement depending on the service provided and the main clauses that impact on the administration of the client account	4

Examination Specification

Each examination paper is constructed from a specification that determines the weightings that will be given to each element. The specification is given below.

It is important to note that the numbers quoted may vary slightly from examination to examination as there is some flexibility to ensure that each examination has a consistent level of difficulty. However, the number of questions tested in each element should not change by more than plus or minus 2.

Element Number	Element	Questions
1	Fundamentals of Client Money and Assets	4
2	Regulatory Structures	6
3	Client Money Fundamentals (CASS 7)	9
4	Controls over Client Money (CASS 7)	6
5	Safe Custody Fundamentals (CASS 6)	5
6	Controls over Safe Custody Assets (CASS 6)	5
7	Governance and Oversight	6
8	When Problems Arise…	5
9	The Client	4
	Total	**50**

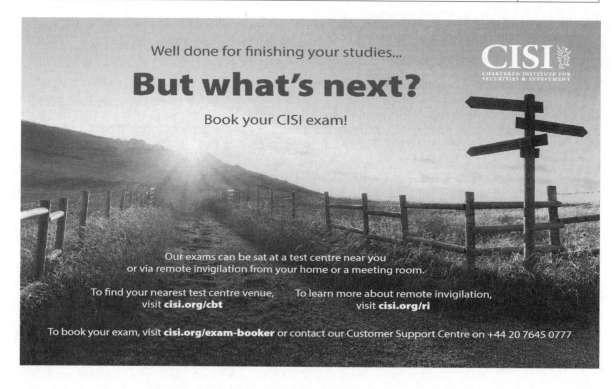

CISI Chartered MCSI Membership can work for you...

Studying for a CISI qualification is hard work and we're sure you're putting in plenty of hours, but don't lose sight of your goal!

This is just the first step in your career; there is much more to achieve!

The securities and investments sector attracts ambitious and driven individuals. You're probably one yourself and that's great, but on the other hand you're almost certainly surrounded by lots of other people with similar ambitions.

So how can you stay one step ahead during these uncertain times?

Entry Criteria for Chartered MCSI Membership

As an ACSI and MCSI candidate, you can upgrade your membership status to Chartered MCSI. There are a number of ways of gaining the CISI Chartered MCSI membership.

A straightforward route requires candidates to have:
- a minimum of one year's ACSI or MCSI membership;
- passed a full Diploma; Certificate in Private Client Investment Advice & Management or Masters in Wealth Management award;
- passed IntegrityMatters with an A grade; and
- successfully logged and certified 12 months' CPD under the CISI's CPD Scheme.

Alternatively, experienced-based candidates are required to have:
- a minimum of one year's ACSI membership;
- passed IntegrityMatters with an A grade; and
- successfully logged and certified six years' CPD under the CISI's CPD Scheme.

Joining Fee:	Current Grade of Membership	Grade of Chartership	Upgrade Cost
	ACSI	Chartered MCSI	£85.00
	MCSI	Chartered MCSI	£30.00

By belonging to a Chartered professional body, members will benefit from enhanced status in the industry and the wider community. Members will be part of an organisation which holds the respect of government and the financial services sector, and can communicate with the public on a whole new level. There will be little doubt in consumers' minds that chartered members of the CISI are highly regarded and qualified professionals and, as a consequence, will be required to act as such.

The Chartered MCSI designation will provide you with full access to all member benefits, including Professional Refresher where there are currently over 100 modules available on subjects including Anti-Money Laundering, Information Security & Data Protection, Integrity & Ethics, and the UK Bribery Act. CISI TV is also available to members, allowing you to catch up on the latest CISI events, whilst earning valuable CPD.

Revision Express

You've bought the workbook... now test your knowledge before your exam.

Revision Express is an engaging online study tool to be used in conjunction with most CISI workbooks.

Key Features of Revision Express:
- Questions throughout to reaffirm understanding of the subject
- Special end-of-module practice exam to reflect as closely as possible the standard you will experience in your exam (please note, however, they are not the CISI exam questions themselves)
- Extensive glossary of terms
- Allows you to study whenever you like, and on any device

IMPORTANT: The questions contained in Revision Express products are designed as aids to revision, and should not be seen in any way as mock exams.

Price per Revision Express module: £35
Price when purchased with the corresponding CISI workbook: £108 (normal price: £119)

To purchase Revision Express:

call our Customer Support Centre on:
+44 20 7645 0777

or visit the CISI's online bookshop at:
cisi.org/bookshop

For more information on our elearning products, contact our Customer Support Centre on +44 20 7645 0777, or visit our website at cisi.org/elearning

Professional Refresher

Self-testing elearning modules to refresh your knowledge, meet regulatory and firm requirements, and earn CPD.

Professional Refresher is a training solution to help you remain up-to-date with industry developments, maintain regulatory compliance and demonstrate continuing learning.

This popular online learning tool allows self-administered refresher testing on a variety of topics, including the latest regulatory changes.

There are over 120 modules available which address UK and international issues. Modules are reviewed by practitioners frequently and new ones are added to the suite on a regular basis.

Benefits to firms:
- Learning and testing can form part of business T&C programme
- Learning and testing kept up-to-date and accurate by the CISI
- Relevant and useful – devised by industry practitioners
- Access to individual results available as part of management overview facility, 'Super User'
- Records of staff training can be produced for internal use and external audits
- Cost-effective – no additional charge for CISI members
- Available for non-members to purchase

Benefits to individuals:
- Comprehensive selection of topics across sectors
- Modules are regularly refreshed and updated by industry experts
- New modules added regularly
- Free for members
- Successfully passed modules are recorded in your CPD log as active learning
- Counts as structured learning for RDR purposes
- On completion of a module, a certificate can be printed out for your own records

The full suite of Professional Refresher modules is free to CISI members, or £250 for non-members. Modules are also available individually. To view a full list of Professional Refresher modules visit:

cisi.org/refresher

If you or your firm would like to find out more, contact our Client Relationship Management team:

+ 44 20 7645 0670
crm@cisi.org

For more information on our elearning products, contact our Customer Support Centre on +44 20 7645 0777, or visit our website at cisi.org/refresher

Professional Refresher

Top 5

SCORM COMPLIANT

Integrity & Ethics
- High-Level View
- Ethical Behaviour
- An Ethical Approach
- Compliance vs Ethics

Anti-Money Laundering
- Introduction to Money Laundering
- UK Legislation and Regulation
- Money Laundering Regulations 2017
- Proceeds of Crime Act 2002
- Terrorist Financing
- Suspicious Activity Reporting
- Money Laundering Reporting Officer
- Sanctions

General Data Protection Regulation (GDPR)
- Understanding the Terminology
- The Six Data Protection Principles
- Data Subject Rights
- Technical and Organisational Measures

Information Security and Data Protection
- Cyber-Security
- The Regulators

UK Bribery Act
- Background to the Act
- The Offences
- What the Offences Cover
- When Has an Offence Been Committed?
- The Defences Against Charges of Bribery
- The Penalties

Latest

Cryptocurrencies
- Bitcoin
- Altcoins
- Central Bank Digital Currency and Cryptofiat
- Trading Cryptocurrencies
- The Impact of Cryptocurrencies

Change Management
- Types of Change
- Change Theories
- The Complexities of Change
- Leading Change
- Key Skills and Competencies

Regulatory Update
- General Regulatory Changes
- Sector Changes

Common Reporting Standard (CRS)
- What is the CRS?
- Implementation and Compliance
- Practical Issues
- The Global Perspective

Cross-Border Investment Services
- The UK System
- Overseas Regulation
- Applicability
- Face-to-Face Meetings
- Distance Communications
- Brexit Implications
- Gifts and Entertainment
- Tax Evasion, Money Laundering, and Terrorist Financing

Operations

Best Execution
- What Is Best Execution?
- Achieving Best Execution
- Order Execution Policies
- Information to Clients & Client Consent
- Monitoring, the Rules, and Instructions
- Best Execution for Specific Types of Firms

Approved Persons Regime
- The Basis of the Regime
- Fitness and Propriety
- The Controlled Functions
- Principles for Approved Persons
- The Code of Practice for Approved Persons

Corporate Actions
- Corporate Structure and Finance
- Life Cycle of an Event
- Mandatory Events
- Voluntary Events

Wealth

Client Assets and Client Money
- Protecting Client Assets and Client Money
- Segregation and Holding
- Due Diligence of Custodians and Banks
- Reconciliations
- Records and Accounts
- CASS Oversight

Investment Principles and Risk
- Diversification
- Factfind and Risk Profiling
- Investment Management
- Modern Portfolio Theory and Investing Styles
- Direct and Indirect Investments
- Socially Responsible Investment
- Collective Investments
- Investment Trusts
- Dealing in Debt Securities and Equities

Banking Standards
- Introduction and Background
- Strengthening Individual Accountability
- Reforming Corporate Governance
- Securing Better Outcomes for Consumers
- Enhancing Financial Stability

Suitability of Client Investments
- Assessing Suitability
- Risk Profiling
- Establishing Risk Appetite
- Obtaining Customer Information
- Suitable Questions and Answers
- Making Suitable Investment Selections
- Guidance, Reports and Record Keeping

International

Foreign Account Tax Compliance Act (FATCA)
- Foreign Financial Institutions
- Due Diligence Requirements
- Reporting
- Compliance

MiFID II
- The Organisations Covered by MiFID II
- The Products Subject to MiFID II
- The Origins of MiFID II
- The Impact of MiFID II
- The Products Covered by MiFID II
- Cross-Border Business Under MiFID II

UCITS
- The Original UCITS Directive
- UCITS III
- UCITS IV
- Non-UCITS Funds
- Latest Developments

cisi.org/refresher

Feedback to the CISI

Have you found this workbook to be a valuable aid to your studies? We would like your views, so please email us at learningresources@cisi.org with any thoughts, ideas or comments.

Accredited Training Partners

Support for exam students studying for the Chartered Institute for Securities & Investment (CISI) qualifications is provided by several Accredited Training Partners (ATPs), including Fitch Learning and BPP. The CISI's ATPs offer a range of face-to-face training courses, distance learning programmes, their own learning resources and study packs which have been accredited by the CISI. The CISI works in close collaboration with its ATPs to ensure they are kept informed of changes to CISI exams so they can build them into their own courses and study packs.

CISI Workbook Specialists Wanted

Workbook Authors

Experienced freelance authors with finance experience, and who have published work in their area of specialism, are sought. Responsibilities include:

- Updating workbooks in line with new syllabuses and any industry developments
- Ensuring that the syllabus is fully covered

Workbook Reviewers

Individuals with a high-level knowledge of the subject area are sought. Responsibilities include:

- Highlighting any inconsistencies against the syllabus
- Assessing the author's interpretation of the workbook

Workbook Technical Reviewers

Technical reviewers to provide a detailed review of the workbook and bring the review comments to the panel. Responsibilities include:

- Cross-checking the workbook against the syllabus
- Ensuring sufficient coverage of each learning objective

Workbook Proofreaders

Proofreaders are needed to proof workbooks both grammatically and also in terms of the format and layout. Responsibilities include:

- Checking for spelling and grammar mistakes
- Checking for formatting inconsistencies

If you are interested in becoming a CISI external specialist call:
+44 20 7645 0609

or email:
externalspecialists@cisi.org

For bookings, orders, membership and general enquiries please contact our Customer Support Centre on +44 20 7645 0777, or visit our website at cisi.org